The Soul's Journey

Blanca:
May God bless your
Souls journey
Bill Tubo

The Soul's Journey

Best Loved Sermons

William E. Nebo

Sursum Corda Press
Livermore, California

Editing by Claudia McCormick
Book Design by Judy Lussie
Cover Design and Photo by Charles Eyler

PRINTED IN THE UNITED STATES OF AMERICA

ISBN 978-0-9799929-0-2

Library of Congress Control Number: 2007937611

Table of Contents

Preface

When the announcement was made that Rev. William "Bill" Nebo would be retiring from the ministerial staff after 34 years at the First Presbyterian Church in Livermore, it served as a call for reminiscing among members of the church. It was not uncommon to hear, "I liked that sermon about the weed whacker," or "After all these years, my son still remembers the sermons about Bill as a child."

Hearing these comments and knowing that Bill would no longer be delivering sermons, we proceeded to investigate the possibility of publishing favorites. Not only did we learn that this endeavor was possible but we found a group of friends who were interested in working with us. In addition to us, this review committee included: Claude and Peggy Burdick, Edward and Connie Clark, Jim and Janie Hodges, Judy Lussie, Art Rodrigues, Robbie See, and Ann Laye.

With the help of the church staff, particularly Joy Fischer and Michele O'Hair, we scanned and copied 526 sermons dating back to 1981. Members of our committee read the sermons and gave each a ranking from which excerpts from these sermons were selected for publication.

We are grateful to members of our committee who served as copy editors. This group included: Claude Burdick, Peggy Burdick, Robbie See, and Larry Burdick.

We want to thank three special individuals who are primarily responsible for this publication: Claudia McCormick who served proficiently as the content editor and Judy and Bill Lussie who served as the mainstay in the publishing phase of this project.

Finally, we wish to thank Chuck Eyler for the cover design, including the photos of Bill and his beloved Border collie, Monty.

It is our hope that these best loved sermons of Bill Nebo will be enjoyed for many years by present and future generations.

Marvin and Mary V. Dickerson,
Sermon Project Co-chairs

Introduction

Though I am the writer of the sermons that are presented here, I am not really the "author". The thoughts, stories, insights, and studies are often borrowed from the lives and minds of others I was privileged to encounter during my journey, and inspired by the living spirit of Christ.

During my ministry, I found that most of what we do well as human beings is not the result of one person's endeavors. Our best insights and creations are often the outcome of that sacred enlightenment that emerges after we have explored the many trials and experiences contributed by others throughout time.

The preaching done from the pages that follow was directed to a living parish, and in many ways formed by that same parish's needs and yearnings as I humbly perceived them. When I wrote the sermons I never dreamed that they would be published, even in a limited way. Without the competent judgment, willingness, and desire of the congregation to gather together these best remembered sermons, they would have remained files on my computer.

I hope that I have given adequate recognition to the sources used in my sermons, and if not, I pray I am forgiven any such innocent oversight, and hope that the sources benefit from the fact that others have found their words helpful enough to be remembered.

It is my prayerful desire that the compassionate love of God I sought to illustrate in my preaching is somehow conveyed to you in the words my beloved congregants chose to publish.

Rev. William E. Nebo

This book is dedicated to several influential people in my life; my brother Jack, whose love sustained me during childhood; to the memory of my late wife Jean, who brought calm and stability to my world; my present family and my wife, Jane for their patience and support; and finally, to the faithful congregation of the First Presbyterian Church of Livermore, fellow travelers on the soul's journey.

Knowing Heaven When You See It

December 23, 2001

As a 10-year-old boy, I knew the stories of Christmas quite well. I knew that they spoke of a love and acceptance I could trust to make my life meaningful forever. Although that was important to me, being a foster kid and sometimes wondering to whom I really belonged, Christmas had an additional significance at that time in my life. I knew that God loved me; Christ was born in a manger in Bethlehem to redeem me and all of humankind. However, all those wonderful truths had become secondary to my love of the Wenmack Aeromight Airplane.

During that season of Advent, I felt twinges of uncomfortable guilt when the Sunday school teacher at our local Baptist church waxed eloquent over the 10 commandments. She seemed to pause over the "honor thy father and mother" commandment and look knowingly at us boys. We would dart glances at each other - the kind of fleeting look that said, "Hey, she must be talking about you, not me." Moving on down the list of commandments, the teacher would put a special emphasis on "Thou shalt not bear false witness" and make a point of saying, "God doesn't want us to be liars".

Luckily for me, the teacher would rush right by "Thou shalt not covet." If she ever stopped there and looked around I would have to confess. Yes, yes! I am a coveter. I covet the Wenmack Aeromite Airplane.

It was a fire engine red; all plastic control-line model airplane powered by a zippy Aeromite .049 engine. I had watched them flying at the local park, the young pilots spinning round endlessly in circles guiding the swift little air craft on two strings attached to a handle. These airborne wonders were the favorite prize of give-away kid programs, which I salivated over, but never won.

That Christmas, when my brother and I went to my aunt and uncle's home to open our presents there was no Wenmack Aeromite Airplane under the tree for me. My brother and I opened up gifts of toy firearms; it was the era when parents didn't shrink from buying these props for playtime for their sons. My cousin Bobby was happy with his trucks and cars, and we were all outside playing catch with the new baseball set when something awesome happened.

The neighbors emerged from their house carrying a Wenmack Aeromite Airplane. I was filled with an envy I could barely keep under control. There before my eyes was the real Christmas I had wanted. The grownups were carrying the plane, while the owner, a kid my age, trailed behind watching in anticipation while his father prepared the airplane for its maiden flight. We all watched from a distance while his Dad and Uncle put the model down in the street, and stretched the control lines onto the lawn.

I stood there paralyzed by my desire to be the one hooking up the battery cables, flipping the propeller around until with a slight pop, the motor would buzz to life.

While an uncle held the plane the boy's father ran to the control handle. The boy stood with his hands over his ears, shrinking back in respectful admiration of that which one day would be his to master. His father motioned the uncle to let go of the airplane and it shot into the air. The airplane did one big, high revolution, as the father tried to anticipate what was up and down while looking into the blinding sun. It was all over very quickly: the airplane plunged straight into the hard asphalt of the street and shattered into a score of small and large shimmering red fragments.

The father and uncle gathered up the pieces, wound the string around the shattered wing remnant, and the whole retinue trooped wordlessly into the house. It had taken all of five minutes.

My brother, that great paragon of empathy, looked at me with feigned shock, and said loudly ... "Daaaa, Whoops!"

And suddenly all of us were laughing so uncontrollably hard that my sides hurt. Part of my laughter was over the fact that for all of its great hold over my life, the Wenmack Aeromite failed to survive Christmas. It wasn't eternal; it didn't even last through Christmas day.

What was eternal was the event itself, the imprint of those moments on our young lives, the imprint of the spontaneous laughter we shared which said life is wonderful, both winning and losing, locked in the invisible bands of kinship, friendship, humor and grace.

I often think of that little boy and wonder if he looks back on that Christmas and laughs about the day his dad smashed his Wenmack Aeromite in less time than it had taken to open the box. God is never in the material things we covet; God is not in the prestigious titles we pursue, or the power we seek. God is in the human connection with one another and with the other beings and tides of our universe. That is when we know heaven.

My brother Jack and I arrive at our fourth and last foster home. Each time we moved, we agreed to allow ourselves to cry for no more than an hour.

God's Will - My Will

May 5, 2001

From the first century until the present time, those of us who have become followers of Jesus Christ know the importance of comprehending what God wants for our lives. What we desire is not necessarily what God desires and often God's plan for us is in conflict with our own wishes.

Discerning the voice of God in our lives is not an easy thing to do. When I discerned the call of God to enter the ministry, I was like Peter, incredulous that I would be asked to make such a fundamental shift in my life. In 1959, going into the ministry was not one of the great respected professions of aspiring young high school students. It was during the Cold War and technology was king. The propaganda of the time promised a rich and rewarding life for people like me who sought a future in electrical engineering.

The last thing I wanted to do was spend my life dealing with the fuzzy outcomes abounding in a people-oriented profession like ministering. A chance reading of the beautiful Thornton Wilder play, **Our Town**, changed all of that. Two characters in the drama, the stage manager and Emily, began to haunt me night after night with deep questions about life, death, meaning, destiny, and the reality of God in my life. Suddenly I could hardly work at the academic subjects that would propel me toward my goal of financial bliss and hardware heaven.

After two tortuous months of trying to regain my assurance that engineering was the right path to take, I decided to get quiet and really listen to what God might want for me to do with my life. I realized that I had been doing everything I could to distract myself from the gnawing thought that there was something urging me to seek a different path from the one my ego wanted to pursue. When I grew quiet and meditative, waiting for holy insight to make the right decision, it came through loud and clear. It was the realization of my worst thoughts. I was not to pursue the lucrative path of new technological discoveries. Instead, I was to enter a profession with low pay, low public recognition at the time, and low respect in the eyes of my family.

When the decision was made, an incredible peace came over me. It was one of those rare times when I actually experienced for a moment the peace that passes understanding.

I came to realize the importance of Christians spending time in quiet reflection, putting away distractions and the voice of ego, culture, peer group, career goals and the like, and really listen for the sometimes startling will of God for their lives.

Spiritual practices throughout time and throughout religious traditions, Christian and otherwise, provide a consistent set of procedures by which a person can increase his or her ability to discern God's will from their own will or the desires of others. How do we do this?

To discern God we have to listen quietly and intently for God's voice. The psalmist echoes this when he tells us that we must be still in order to know God. This is why quiet meditation that seeks to clear the mind of all thoughts is a necessary discipline for anyone who wants to consistently seek to discern God. Without this exercise, the mind and ego will continually present its own agenda as if it were God's agenda. One way to tell if we are discerning God's voice or our own is to check to see how much we find God urging us to do what we really wanted to do in the first place. When we listen for God we need to discard our own agenda, and listen to the spirit who lives within us, who knows the end from the beginning, and will lead us in the right direction.

The promise of God to be with us even to the close of the age is Jesus' promise to accompany us into the realm of listening with a detachment from our agenda. For, once we do disengage from our agenda we can view our lives as a series of events that are not judged negatively or positively. Instead, we see them through the eyes of the grace of God and whether what appears is straight or twisted, the power of God can use it to make something wonderful and meaningful.

We grow quiet by meditative practice. Learning this is easy if we spend time each day practicing this discipline; five minutes a day will bring stunning results.

Listening for God, discerning God's will, is a matter of listening reflectively, meditatively, and quietly to the messages of our life. This means we have to stop long enough and grow non-judgmentally quiet enough in the presence of the Holy Spirit to review our lives truthfully in detail. Journaling is a good way to do this. Reflecting with a very good confidant is another way to do this. The way not to do it is to neglect the process and simply live life concentrating on just a few notions about your journey.

Listening for God's will is also a matter of listening for God in the lives of others. This means cultivating a life long habit of really listening to people with both one's head and one's heart. The art of hearing people is not trivial. Too often we listen through the filter of our predispositions and prejudices and we miss the presence of God's wisdom and guidance in the lives of others passing before us. But we make ourselves deaf to their wisdom by turning up the volume on our assumptions.

Jed Harris, who was one of the producers of the original production of *Our Town* was once convinced that he was losing his hearing. So he went to a specialist who gave him a check-up. Pulling out a gold watch the specialist asked if Harris could hear it ticking. Harris said of course. The specialist walked to the door, held up the watch and asked if he could hear it now. Harris said again, "yes". The doctor walked out the door into the next room and said loudly, "Can you hear it now?" Harris said after listening intently, "Yes."

The doctor then said, "Mr. Harris, there is nothing wrong with your hearing. You just don't listen."

Listen to your life. Listen deeply, patiently, to all of the people who are God's gifts to your life. Listen to them whether they are your friends or not, whether they are your social class or not, whether they are your intellectual peers or not. Listen patiently, reverently, forgivingly to the stories and dramas of your own life and the lives of others.

Listen with faith and you will discern the still small voice of God.

Humble Power

 My Foster father was not a man of great religious zeal. He would go to church and testify to his beliefs if pressed, but he felt uncomfortable doing so. As I grew older I became aware of some of the patterns of his life that made him feel so uncomfortable seeing himself as "holy".

He believed the state of holiness was for people better than he was. Once he told me that he thought I would make a good minister, because I was such a calming person. I suppose he was trying to tell me that my holiness made me worthy for such a calling. It was the farthest thing from my mind.

When I was in the 5th grade, my foster dad gave me a lesson in woodworking. I had always admired his ability to work with wood and had wanted to be like him. The lesson was a chance for me to absorb the master craftsmanship that I so treasured in my foster Dad's life.

He opened up his folding ruler and began to explain that a good wood worker always measured things in order to carefully plan his work. He also explained that the ruler he was letting me use that day was very special because my foster mother's dad had given it to him. I had always called this person DAD, and he was one of the most revered heroes of my life. It was with shaking hands that I received the sacred ruler.

I spent a long time laying out my project, unfolding and folding the ruler, teaching myself how to make it lay flat with the work, or to form a kind of square. My brother noticed what I was doing and decided to join in. He approached me from behind, asking if he could try the ruler. Turning around to hand it to him, I didn't notice that he was approaching me at a pretty fast pace.

Misjudging his distance from me, I jammed the extended end of the ruler into his chest, and with a sickening snap, one of the extensions broke off.

I was horrified. There was no good way to explain what had happened, I thought. No matter what I said, the fact was that I had been careless and broken the ruler. When my foster dad came into the garage shortly after the mishap and saw the ruler, he exploded. His anger was soon muffled when he realized that cursing was only making me cry. So he swept up the pieces of the ruler and started out of the garage. My mom came running to see what was going on and I heard my dad say, "I just can't trust these kids with anything."

My mom cut him off sharply, saying "Now don't you go saying that ... he didn't mean to break it and if you didn't want to take the chance of having it damaged, you shouldn't have given it to him."

In spite of her words, my dad was too infuriated to do anything but sullenly go into the house.

For days afterward I would not go into the garage and I would not resume my project because going near it made me remember that awful day. One day my foster dad asked me why I wasn't finishing my wood project and I didn't answer.

My mom was near, and she peered at me like she was looking into my head. Then she said to my dad, "You fool; he's not doing it because you got so angry at him about Dad's ruler."

I never before or since saw my foster dad look so broken or sorry. I was looking at the floor, trying not to drown in my guilt, when he came up to me, got down on his knees so I couldn't avoid his gaze, put both of his big hands on my shoulders and said, "I'm sorry for getting angry, I really didn't mean to act so unkind. Dad's ruler is just a ruler, I can always get another one, and I have the rest of his ruler. You mean more to me than any ruler or anything else in my life."

There were tears in his eyes and he was struggling not to choke when he spoke. He hugged me, and a burden lifted from my shoulders.

A day or so later my foster dad got another ruler and made sure that I saw it and ushered me to the garage so I could use it. He showed me where he kept it stored and said I could use it any time.

When I grew older there were things I learned about my foster dad that he thought would never see the light of day. I realized that these eclipsed parts of him were what always made him feel inadequate in his own sense of 'holiness'. I suppose that his own self-judgment were what prevented him from fully manifesting the holiness in him.

The new ruler made a great difference in my relationship to him. It was the holy forgiveness and love that I saw in his eyes when he let me know that he loved me more than Dad's ruler. I always saw the holiness in my Dad, rather than his lack of it. Even later when he did things that made me mad or impatient with him, I always believed in the holiness I saw in him that day in fifth grade ... and loved him.

Christ sees in us that kind of holiness, even when we don't feel it and are not expressing our holiness because of our doubts about its existence. Jesus saw holiness in John the Baptizer, who felt unworthy to baptize Jesus. When he discerned this in John, he bid John to not let him be prevented from expressing holiness either by custom, or feelings of inadequacy, or some human pecking order.

Christ invites us to manifest our holiness in places where we might think it isn't welcome. Such as in our relationship with our employer or employees or coworkers; in the corporate boardroom; in our political life; in our neighborhood; in our shopping and interaction with salespeople and clerks: in our dealing with friends and family; in our treatment of ourselves.

I still have the ruler that my dad bought to replace the one I broke. When I had visited him in the home where he lived, his memory forever lost to Alzheimer's disease, the ruler was really the only thing of his possessions that I wanted to keep. To me, it is a powerful symbol of his holiness in my life.

That same holiness is in us, my friends. Yes, we do possess the power to work miracles, if we will only access it in faith and action.

Pretension Prevention

October 30, 2005

In 1968 I was ordained to the Gospel ministry and called to be the Assistant Pastor to the First United and Portalhurst Presbyterian Churches of San Francisco. For four years I had worked at First Church as a Seminary Assistant, but now I was working for the first time as a full time pastor and could write 'Rev' in front of my name. But most importantly, I was given a uniform. I had a brand new robe and a wonderfully colorful academic hood that served as authoritative pieces of liturgical gear.

Just after acquiring my uniform, a call came from a large San Francisco mortuary for a Presbyterian pastor to do a funeral. Since my boss was out of town, I took the call. The mortician told me that it was a small funeral and would involve internment at a cemetery in a neighboring city. I could either ride in the hearse or get into the procession with my own car. I chose driving in the procession, thinking my 1957 VW hippy bus would appear appropriately humble in the tiny knot of cars the small service would produce.

I arrived at the mortuary early as I was anxious to publicly debut my new life of uniformed authority and credentialed title, and I didn't want to spoil any of it by being late. I donned my priestly gear and paced the floor in the service lobby with sophisticated patience. A nun passed by and commented on how the red in my stole was quite stunning.

Appreciating the adulation, I tried to mutter something appropriately wise in return but what came out was something like: "Aa gee aahh ... thanks mam, er, aa, sister. Mother?" I hadn't yet developed the quick wit suggested by my liturgical garb. I wish I had known what this moment of awkwardness portended.

The mortician arrived and ushered me down a dark hallway. We entered the chapel through a side door. I instinctively took a step back. The room was huge! Imposingly so! The crowd was enormous, people standing in the aisles, and it seemed, hanging from the icons on the wall. I wasn't used to really large crowds yet. For a moment I considered slipping back out the door and through the little hallway and back to my old life as an innocent seminary intern. Back there I didn't have to face sophisticated San Franciscans wearing expensive suits and furs, and clearly sporting more life experience than I could comprehend at the tender age of 26.

The mortician was standing in the door, looking at me expectantly, as though I really knew what I was doing. My sophisticated clerical garb was broadcasting a great lie to everyone watching this young pastor with the Afro haircut. "Let us pray" I croaked, and the service began, ready or not.

Somehow I made it through the main service. I was glad my clothing was really absorbent so that the sweat didn't collect in my shoes. As the family and mourners left for the cemetery, I fled to my 1957 VW bus, cursing the decision not to ride in the hearse. In contrast to the rows of sleek late model cars, my VW bus looked like something driven by a derelict that was crashing the party for the refreshments. All of the sleek new cars purred leaving the lot in procession, while my van clattered away like a sewing machine.

Somewhere on the freeway leading to the cemetery, my little van began to fall behind the procession. One car after another glided passed me, until I was the tail end of the procession. By the time I arrived in the area, not one car of the huge procession was in view. I had the accelerator peddle floored. In fact, I was making a small depression in the thin metal of the floor trying to push it further to obtain more speed.

I chugged up the final hill of the cemetery and found everyone parked in long lines on both sides of the road. People were milling about in their expensive suits, looking perplexed, looking for the young minister in the Afro and the pretty liturgical stole that was nowhere to be seen. I had to park at the very end of the huge line of cars and run up the hill, robes flying. When I finally got to the grave site, in this case a niche for cremated remains, I was gasping for air. The expectant crowd had been waiting and wanted to start immediately. Without giving me a chance to fully recover they gathered round me their eyes saying, "So, let's get this going Rev."

I began, "puff, puff, 'let us pray' puff puff."

After it was over, I gave condolences to the relatives I had never really met and nearly ran to the van, leaped in, tried to make a U-turn without revving the engine too much and drove off.

To this day I have no idea who I buried; whether that person was a male or female, young or old. My experience with pretension clouded everything. It was a great lesson about pretension and how it gets in the way.

When Jesus was around people in holy garb like I was at the funeral he noticed that there were old and young people whose perceptive ability was clouded by pretension. Some of the Pharisees and rabbis in his life liked to be known by their titles. They enjoyed the special places where they were invited to sit at feasts and celebrations and gatherings. They enjoyed the deference with which people treated them. They especially liked the idea that their office made them a little better than other folk - a little more powerful and a little more privileged.

Some even resented it when those privileges were overlooked by some one who was not knowledgeable about how they should be treated or regarded. We know that this sort of human pretension seemed to get under Jesus's skin. It wasn't that the religious elite were so much worse about being pretentious than others. What bothered Jesus was that they were the representatives of God, who had no great love of human pretension. Given how Jesus lived, and died, and rose again, and the way he expressed gracious love for even street people who occasionally crashed the parties of the wealthy, his life made the point that God in all God's power and Glory would not crowd into line telling the host angrily, "Do you know who I am?"

From the book of Joshua we learn that when the children of Israel were about to enter the land of promise, there was no Moses to strike the waters of the Jordan and make them part. The thought that without one special anointed leader they were not worthy of God's presence was left behind in a grave containing the body of Moses, a grave hidden somewhere at the edge of the wilderness. It was wise to have it hidden. That way no one could make a relic of his bones, claiming that they, and not God in each individual, gave God's power, favor, confidence, and purpose to the community of faith.

So it was that Joshua was the instructor of the priests. The 12 representatives of every member of the tribes of Israel whose feet touched the Jordan's waters made the waters cease to flow south toward the Negev. The point was made. The power of God that changes things is invested in all of the people, not just one individual. Even Joshua, the great leader of the Exodus, was no more worthy to convey the power to part the waters of the Jordan than twelve nameless representatives of every person entering the land of promise.

One of the things we celebrate on Reformation Sunday is this notion that God is not a God of pretentiousness. God does not play favorites, valuing one of God's children over another. We remember this when we read of how Jesus was annoyed at religious people who allowed their pretensions to blind them to the real task of bearing to the world the love and grace of God.

Pretension blinds us to the real gifts of God. It blinds us to the things others have to tell us about the world, ourselves, God. It blinds us to the presence of treasures buried in those things and people that are judged to be beneath our pretensions and not worthy of our serious consideration.

Jesus was once invited to a dinner at the home of an important Pharisee. While the appetizers were being served, a street person wandered into the courtyard where the party was being held. She saw Jesus, approached him and fell on her knees before him. She wept, washing his feet with her tears and wiping them with her hair. The pretentious felt that this behavior should be shunned by people of importance. The Pharisees watched her and Jesus with obvious disdain.

Jesus let the woman continue. When she had finished he gave her a blessing. In so doing, Jesus Christ gives us the promise that God sees us as we are, beyond all pretensions. And that is the person God calls his beloved.

Sursum Corda

May 20, 1984

When I was in college I went to Tijuana, Mexico, with a work caravan from my home church to build a medical clinic in the hills on the outskirts of that city. There I experienced the poverty and tenuousness of life that I know now is the plight of so many people on earth. I also experienced there the universal hunger for God -- a hunger that remains even when stomachs are filled and bodies are clothed. The experience connected me forever with people and conditions I never thought possible.

While we were there I worked with a crew, which was assigned the task of constructing a rock wall of mortar and native stone from a local quarry. I had never built anything like this before and I was mystified at how rocks of so many different sizes and shapes would ever make a wall. I was not alone in my puzzlement.

Consequently the work crew spent hours surveying piles of rock, looking first for the larger rocks for the bottom of the wall and smaller rocks as we layered up to the top of the 3.5 foot structure. We looked for rocks that roughly went together, that would require little mortar.

As a result we worked tediously long hours in the hot sun putting the wall together as though it were a puzzle.

Later, a Mexican builder told us, "the rocks are really the same family; it doesn't matter if a big rock lives next to a little one. It is the balance and bracing of small and large linked together with as much mortar as it takes to anchor the rocks that makes a wall go up."

The first book of Peter was written in a time when the apostle was trying to make people fit together in a task, much like we were trying to fit rocks together in a wall in Mexico. However, he was constructing a living wall of individuals which would connect with other walls to build one structure called the church. It needed to be an especially strong wall, because of the great pressure he knew it had to withstand. He also knew that if he had to build like the Mexican builder, seeing this tremendously diverse group of people fit together in a mutually supporting way, he could not allow the wasted time and effort and weakness that would result from trying to stratify rocks and match them together.

As always, the writer of this book is disputed. But there is strong evidence that this book is what it purports to be, the writing of the apostle Peter to (as verses 1 and 2 of the first chapter says) all those living among foreigners in the Dispersion of Pontus, Galatia, Cappadocia, Asia and Bithynia. In short, districts located in the northeast corner of Asia Minor.

This book was written to prepare the people for great hardship, a series of blows of great proportions. It was not written in vain. The blows came from the hand of the emperor, Nero.

Before 64 AD, Judaism was considered a permitted religion by the Roman government, and Jews were permitted to worship in their own way. Since Rome was not really aware of how separate Christianity had become from its parent Judaism, it simply allowed Christians to worship as though they were Jewish.

All that changed with the events that began on the 19th of July in the year 64. This was the year that the great fire of Rome broke out and the entire city was in danger of being wiped out. The fire burned for three days and three nights; it was checked. Then it broke out again with redoubled violence.

The Roman populace had no doubt who was responsible for it. They put the blame fairly and squarely on Nero, the emperor. Nero had a passion for building; and they believed that he had deliberately taken steps to obliterate Rome so that he might build it again.

The resentment of the people was bitter. Nero had to divert suspicion from him so a scapegoat had to be found. He found them, weak unarmed, under suspicion anyway -- the Christians.

Even Tacitus, the Non-Christian Roman historian who wrote of Nero's actions expresses alarm at the mindless slaughter of these innocent people.

In his *Annals* he writes:

> "Mockery of every sort was added to their (Christians) deaths. Covered with the skins of beasts, they were torn by dogs and perished, or were nailed to crosses, or were doomed to the flames and burned to serve as nightly illumination when daylight had expired. Nero offered his gardens for the spectacle, and was exhibiting a show in the circus, while he mingled with the people in the dress of a charioteer, or stood aloft on a car. Hence, even for criminals who deserve extreme and exemplary punishment, there arose a feeling of compassion;

for, it was not, as it seemed, for the public good, but to glut one man's cruelty that they were being destroyed."

Sulipicius Severus, the Christian historian, also wrote of this event saying:

"In this way, cruelty first began to be manifested against the Christians. Afterwards, too, their religion was prohibited by laws, that were enacted; and by edicts openly set forth it was proclaimed unlawful to be a Christian.

After the Neronic wave had passed over the capital, the wash of it was felt on the far shores of the provinces; the dramatic publicity of the punishment must have spread the name of Christian far and wide over the entire empire; the provincials would soon hear of it and when they desired a similar outburst at the expense of the loyal Christians, all that they needed was a proconsul to gratify their wishes, and some outstanding disciple to serve as a victim."

In the end it was not Roman law that threatened Christians, but rather lynch law.

To Christians in the provinces, Peter wrote a letter that said what we think and feel and believe about life is going to be challenged. We must now remember who we are and what we are about lest we fall apart when the storm comes raging to our shores.

What were we before we became joined to Christ? We were people who lay around like a pile of rocks, without connection to each other. Somehow it seemed we should be joined together, but all we saw was the discordant nature of life full of strife and selfish competition; families set against families, led by people with an unholy attitude that left us just a pile of rubble rather than a strong structure of inter-connected people joined in one purpose and relationship.

Indeed, the philosophers of the day talked about the family of humanity, but it was all words that had little to do with the common people who were daily trodden under the sandals of the powerful and the favored and even the learned.

In echoing the words of Isaiah and Hosea, Peter tells the flock in the provinces that the coming dangerous times make it more necessary than ever to band together. He reminds them that before they became joined in Christ, they were like so many stones lying in a pile, all knowing they had some potential for something greater, but realizing it didn't mean much as they lay loose in the pile.

God, says Peter, called all of you to be more than just rocks lying around in a pile. In fact, when you were just lying in a pile, life was pretty dull and meaningless and unfulfilling. Even those of you who were rich, found your riches just made you pretty stones in the pile. You were well fed, well groomed, well appointed, but troubled by the nagging question, what was this all for?

Then Christ appeared for us all, called us to build a structure with him as the chief corner stone. What keeps us together is the mortar of God's love, copiously thrown between the cracks and crevices and holes and gaps that exist between us because we indeed are not identical.

Peter writes that the people are the royal priesthood. William Barclay points out that there are two characteristics of the priest that Peter wanted to inspire the Christians of all ages to emulate. The first grows out of the very roots of the word "priest" which is "pontifex" in Latin, meaning a bridge builder. So the word "priest" or "pontifex" refers to one who builds a bridge to God, giving access to God's grace and mercy and love and fulfillment to himself and others.

Second, the priest is one who makes offerings to God, sacrifices in the old dispensations, if you will. In the case of Christendom, the offering is the offering of the self in the service of the kingdom.

The royal priesthood concept says to us that God is making a structure that will allow humankind to access his love and the very heart of the meaning of all life. The structure is composed of people who have realized that in order for the kingdom to come, they must become connected to other people in God's love. This will provide a strong and coherent and lasting connection to that corner-stone that proclaimed God's grace, His Son.

You must not be found as just a pile of strong, pretty, large and small stones, says Peter. If you are, you will be quickly dispersed by the flood that is about to collide with you.

Peter's message is timeless. We often treat our relationship to planet-wide Christendom as though we were either loose stones, or unconnected walls. We lie in the pile waiting for the right fit to come along in the wall, or when we allow ourselves to finally find someplace in the wall, we refuse to apply any mortar. We want to make sure that these rocks around us are our type, speak our language, practice our politics, and have our social standing, education, and child-rearing practices. We want to lie in here with the power of gravity alone, to make sure that when you fit us in, we really fit.

Let me tell you to build any meaningful structure for the sake of God, such a process of picky individualism is going to lead us to grief. We will waste people who lie unattached in the pile because those already in place only see the perfect fit they think they deserve.

The resulting structure will perhaps be handsome, but unsound against controversy, and like other parts of the structure, it will soon think it exists for itself.

So it is that many American Protestants do not feel the agony of their brothers and sisters in Latin America who are Catholic. So it is that we have developed transient Christians always willing to judge their fit in the wall of the kingdom by how it feels to them rather than what strength and integrity it brings to the structure.

So it is that we baptize our children, tell them that they are children of God, ply their need for meaning and place with stories of the great people of the faith. We need to go further and let them know that their identity as the coveted building blocks of God's kingdom means they need to find a place to be mortared into the wall. We cannot be weakly glued in place by God's love, ready to jump out when the preacher says what we don't like, or when we realize that the rocks near us are different from us.

We do not do this by just being Presbyterians, unable and/or unwilling to realize in our core that we are a part of the body of Christ that is bigger than just Presbyterianism. We are also Catholic and Coptic, Russian and Greek Orthodox, Baptist and Episcopalian. When things happen to these parts of the Christian structure, they happen to us as well. That is how God intended this building of his to go together.

There is no significance to being the building stones of God's kingdom if we just lie around in the pile telling our children how good it is to shine in the sun and view the wall from a distance. What good is a lone brick to a stonemason unless he finds a place for it in a wall?

Where are you in the wall? Are you in the pile waiting to find your place in the wall? Are you in the wall by gravity only, hoping no one not your type gets shoved in next to you? Are you perhaps too wed to the idea of being in the American part of the wall, the western part, and the Capitalist or Socialist part of the wall? Are you in need of the mortar of God's love placed in the spaces between you and the others around you?

Before I went to Mexico as a college student, I had a very limited view of the Christian structure and a limited sense of where I fit. But watching the man build a wall, teaching me kindly of my ignorance, I learned a more valuable lesson than the lesson of masonry. I learned that his Catholic perspective and struggles are also mine and I should be eternally grateful for the God who made us brothers and sisters glued together with the mortar of His love. I suddenly see the masonry of God's linking of human beings stretching across the planet and I realize how much I am a part of it. It gives me hope. It can do the same for you if you will let it.

Blasphemy

February 23, 2003

When I was young and my classmates said things they meant to be harmful to me it was the custom to repeat the familiar rhyme, "Sticks and stones can break my bones, but names will never hurt me." The idea here was that whatever terrible things a person said about you or someone else, the words should be dealt with coolly and not with a lot of angry excitement.

But when I got older I discovered that this axiom didn't cover all occasions. For instance there were certain comments said aloud that resulted in my mother washing my mouth out with soap. These remarks were considered "filthy" and hence the cleaning agent treatment. But there were other things that when said, elicited more serious responses.

In an earlier time in our society, profanity was considered blasphemy. Now, we may not be able to tell profanity from ordinary conversation. Blasphemy is generally thought of as a statement or act that offends God. So in the present day what would we consider as blasphemy before God? Can specific words be considered blasphemous to God? Would certain thoughts or expressed ideas be considered blasphemous or do they have to include specific actions that violate what we believe to be the person of God?

In Jesus' day, blasphemy against people meant abusive

speech, personal mockery. It also meant mistaking the true nature of God, violating or doubting God's power, or assuming God's prerogatives. Blasphemy was taken very seriously in Jesus' day. One of the commandments instructs that the name of God should not be taken in vain. We often use this to condemn cursing, but in the ancient text the intent was to ban the use of the name of Yahweh in the attempt to gain power through magic ritual. This was seen as "using God" and that was considered desecration of God's name. The penalty for blasphemy was harsh. Leviticus directed that blasphemy should be punished by stoning. This was what happened to Steven after someone cried out that the content of his speech was blasphemy. It is still taken seriously among some religious communities today.

Because of the gravity of blasphemy, the scribes were surprised to hear Jesus say to the four men and the paralytic they had let down through the roof for him to cure, "Son, your sins are forgiven." The belief of the day was that all illness was a result of sin. Here is what William Barclay says about this passage in his *Daily Bible Study Series on the book of Mark:*

> "When they heard Jesus say to the man that his sins were forgiven, it came as a shattering shock. It was an essential of the Jewish faith that only God could forgive sins. For any man to claim to do so was to insult God; that was blasphemy and the penalty for blasphemy was death by stoning. It was their own firm belief that sin and sickness were indissolubly linked together. A sick man was a man who had sinned. So Jesus asked them, whether is it easier to say to this man, 'Your sins are forgiven,' or to say, 'Get up and walk?' Any charlatan could say, 'Your sins are forgiven.' There was no possibility of ever demonstrating whether his words were effective or

not; such a statement was completely un-checkable. But to say, 'Get up and walk' was to say something whose effectiveness would either be proved or disapproved there and then. So Jesus said in effect: 'You say that you have no right to forgive sins? You hold as a matter of believe that if this man is ill he is a sinner and he cannot be cured till he is forgiven? Very well, then, watch this!' So Jesus spoke the word and the man was cured.

On their own stated beliefs, the man could not be cured, unless he was forgiven. Therefore, he WAS cured. Therefore he WAS forgiven. Therefore, Jesus' claim to forgive sin MUST be true."

Mark's logic is that of the early church. Apparently it was lost on the seriously devout religious folk who could not get over the notion that anyone who declared God's forgiveness was acting as if he were God, usurping God's power. It was tantamount to taking the name of God in vain.

Jesus was saying that there was a side of God that was not as evident in the strictures of the Old Law that was prevalent with harsh measures such as the stoning of Blasphemers. Jesus was saying that he was among people to give witness to the loving and forgiving nature and righteous nature of God. The laws about stoning blasphemers, killing sorcerers and banning people from temple worship were part of a view of God that Jesus was correcting.

William Barclay writes about an essayist named Lewis Hind who in one of his essays tells of the day that he truly discovered the soul of his father. He had always admired and respected his father, but he had always been more than a little afraid of him. One hot, drowsy day he sat in church with his father and grew sleepier and sleepier. He could not keep his eyes open and as waves of sleep engulfed him his head nodded forward. He saw his father's arm go up and he was sure that his father was going to shake or strike him. Then he saw his father smile gently and put his arm round his shoulder. He cuddled the lad to himself so that he might rest more comfortably and held him close with the clasp of love. That day Lewis Hind discovered that his father was not as he had thought him to be and that his father truly loved him.

This is what Jesus did for us in our relationship to God. This is why we have a prayer of confession led by a human pastor or lay person; it doesn't matter. At the end of the prayer the human being is empowered by faith in this nature of God to assure us that all we honestly bring before God to be forgiven is forgiven. Whatever is bound on earth is bound in heaven.

Obviously, some of the authorities witnessing what Jesus did had a difficult time getting around this radical idea. They had been taught that telling people that God forgave them was blasphemy, and that God was a harsh judge who would punish for such usurpation of His power.

I was once accused of blasphemy for something I said while preaching. It happened while I was trying to hold my life together while my wife's cancer grew worse and thinking about what to say to the people attending worship was a matter of rummaging among the most essential truths of life and death. I don't remember exactly what I said, but I mentioned the fact that Buddha or Mohammad had said something similar to the teaching of Jesus about grace, mercy, and forgiveness. I had found it tremendously comforting that what Jesus said about the nature of God's compassion was discoverable in the world by people of other faiths.

After the church service, as I was standing near the communion table alone, a woman who was new to me approached. She said she wanted me to know that she had never been in a church when a pastor blasphemed the name of Jesus by mentioning Him in the same sermon with words sympathetic to the teachings of heretics like Mohammad. I suppose this was for my edification just in case I had forgotten that quoting sages of other faiths in the presence of Christ was really a bad thing. I wondered where she would have gotten this notion. However, there was no invitation to respond. She spun on her heel and stalked away from me clearly not wanting to hear another word from my blasphemous lips.

Indeed, what we disagreed upon is not that there is something called blasphemy, human abuse of the name of God, but rather just what constitutes blasphemy. I began to think about just what I would consider blasphemous. And in thinking it over I came to the conclusion that I would have to consult all I have learned about the nature of God over my 60 years of life and try to come to some helpful conclusions. In doing this I remember that Christ often called God a "parent", and urged us to do so as well.

If I put on my "father hat" and ask myself what could my children do in my "name", that, would make me so angry I would want them put to death?

I concluded that I would not get upset about anything my kids said about me. I have faith that in the end I will win back their love and respect, no matter what name they call me or what they might in their anger and frustration say about me. However, what would get me excited enough to want to intervene is if they used my name, my reputation, and my authority to do harm and bring hurt to others. That would be using their father's name in vain indeed.

I think that any time we rise up in religious indignation and in the name of God proclaim someone in error, (or imply that we are doing so), we are intent upon delivering a self-righteous blow and we mean to bring pain. Therefore, if we believe in the nature of God that Jesus demonstrated on the day he healed the paralytic, we must be open to a reply and a dialogue. If not, then forget delivering the blow. Christians do not use the authority of God's righteousness as a hit and run weapon. In fact, given the nature of God we discover in the life of Christ, I would say that God's name is only evoked for acts leading to reconciliation and healing, never punishment. For the religious authorities of Jesus' ancient world, forgiving in the name of God was blasphemy. For me in the post-resurrection world in which we live, punishing in the name of God is blasphemy. Punish in our own names, but leave God out of it.

This is not a foreign concept to our faith or a clever twisting of thought. Jesus said clearly "Love your enemies, do good to those who hate you." He said "Vengeance is mine, says the Lord. GOD will repay."

Here is an illustration from our nation's past leadership. I greatly respect what President Wilson tried to do for the nation and world at the beginning of the 20th century. He was a devout Presbyterian. He worked for a world of peace and freedom for all. Yet he had a belief that God had ordained him to be president. So when he was asked to compromise on certain points, he said, "God save us from compromise." This caused him to prefer defeat over modestly accommodating his political opponents because he felt one did not compromise with God. I think that appropriating God's name for one's point of view to that extent borders upon blasphemy.

I would pray that we would remember the story of Jesus healing the paralytic and its lessons on the right use of the name of God and the wrong sense of blasphemy. I would hope that we would have the courage to keep in our hearts and minds what Jesus taught us to do when we deal with our enemies. But I needn't remind you of this; you remember, don't you?

When my foster parents took us to the mountains, it was the first time we saw snow. I would walk and fall down and the snow would get in my shoes. It was cold!

Using the Best Crutch

August 12, 2001

In his book, *Following Jesus Without Embarrassing God*, Tony Campolo writes about the meaning and importance of prayer in Christian life. He says,

"When my cynical friends chide me and say, 'You use prayer as a crutch, Campolo, because you don't feel strong enough to face up to what your life is all about,' I can only answer, 'Of course!' Those who believe that they are self-sufficient are, on the one hand, people who don't think they need prayer, and on the other hand, people who are most deluded. To these cynics I can only say, 'Your time will come. And when it does, the good news is that God will be there waiting and willing to carry you through the valley of the shadow of death."

D.L. Moody once said, "I'd rather be able to pray than be a great preacher; Jesus Christ never taught his disciples how to preach, but only how to pray."

I readily agree with Moody, and Tony Campolo. It is certainly true that prayer is indeed a crutch, a support for us in our spiritual feebleness and wounded states. It has sustained me in the darkest of my hours, and guided me in my most perplexing times. Just as I would be foolish not to use a crutch when trying to heal a broken leg, I would be equally foolish in not using the spiritual crutch of prayer to support me when parts of my spiritual life are broken or wounded.

When the disciples asked Jesus how to pray he gave them the words of what we know as the Lord's Prayer. This prayer is rich with the desire for a close relationship with God. The Lord's Prayer begins by recognizing the awesome power and holiness of God. That having been done, the prayer expresses the desire of the petitioner to surrender their future to God. The prayer then asks that God provide the Spiritual food (daily bread) for the individual to sustain their spiritual life. It asks that the impediments of misguided action and thought, the temptation to go another way, be revealed for what they are and avoided.

Prayer is not a trivial matter in the New Testament. It is a serious privilege, which has been given to mere humans on this tiny planet, caught in the gravity of a nondescript star of the Milky Way. Harry Emerson Fosdick once said about prayer, "Our failure to think of prayer as a privilege may be partly due to the fact that we can pray any time. The door to prayer is open so continuously that we fail to avail ourselves of an opportunity which is always there."

The scripture tells us to pray determinedly. Jesus told the story of the man who would give his friend the bread he needed if the man persisted in asking. Notice that Jesus uses bread in the example. Just as the Lord's Prayer speaks of "daily bread" as a way of speaking of daily spiritual nourishment, I have no doubt that Jesus intended parallel meaning for the use of bread in this parable. He is saying do not give up when you are seeking your spiritual fulfillment. Tony Campolo also says in his book what he believes prayer is not. The first thing he points out is that prayer is not magic. He writes that magic is an attempt to control the supernatural powers so that people get what they want. Prayer, on the other hand, is a process wherein people spiritually surrender so that they might become instruments through which the supernatural powers can do their work.

Reducing prayer to magic trivializes God. I remember hearing someone say once that she was cooking a gourmet dinner for an important gathering in her home, and she was in a frenzy over whether what was on her stovetop would finish cooking in time. So she prayed spreading her hands over the top of the steaming, lid covered fry pan. Of course, everything turned out fine, except for her concept of frivolous praying.

Campolo writes of a similar experience.

> "A lady I know told me that her washing machine would not start one day, so she prayed, and God healed her washing machine." I don't want to join the army of cynics out there, but I do have some questions to ask about a God who heals washing machines but doesn't give healing to a godly single mother I know who only wants to be cured from cancer so that her three small children will have their mother.

Just as prayer is not magic, it does not require magic formulas. There are no magic words, names, incantations or rituals which make one form of expression more potent that another. When Jesus told us that if we prayed in His name, He would give us what we asked for (John 14:13), He was talking about something far deeper than reciting a religious formula. That kind of thing would reduce prayer to cheap magic. Instead, He was telling us that, if our prayers are to be effective, we must grow into people who are so like Jesus that our prayer will be an expression of His concerns and love."

The second thing that prayer is not is that it is not something that works if you are extra good or extra spiritual. This means that it doesn't matter if you are pastor, or bishop, or 'well known' spiritual leader when it comes to prayer. Campolo writes,

"I really get ticked off with those holier than thou people, who suggest that they get answers to prayer because they are more spiritual than others. For those arrogant members of the God Squad to suggest to that single mother dying of cancer that, if only she were as 'wonderful' as they were, then healing would be automatic, sickens me. The end result was that these Job like 'comforters' only added guilt to the suffering of this dying mother who faced leaving her small children alone in the world."

Prayer is meant to be the strengthening agent for one's passages into greater and greater depths in spiritual understanding and comprehension. It works most on the humble heart, the poor in spirit, as Jesus called them in his Sermon on the Mount. Since its primary effects upon us are spiritual rather than physical, its efficacy is best experienced by the heart that is honest, unencumbered by ego, and ready to listen rather than speak.

The third thing that it is not, says Campolo, is something you can understand. Not long ago a double blind experiment was conducted using an objective, scientific method to see if there was any truth to the belief that prayer aids in healing. The experiment yielded results, which indicated that people who were administered prayer, healed at a better rate than those not prayed for. Of course this caused a good deal of furor. The scientist was criticized for the fact that he was a practicing Christian, even though he was careful not to allow his personal belief system to influence his method, analysis, data collection and conclusion. In short, prayer isn't going to be helped by scientific analysis, and it isn't going to be stopped by it.

To those who disbelieve in its power in their lives I can only suggest that they try it for themselves. But that may be difficult, because for prayer to have its greatest effects one must pray earnestly, personally, and about one's own journey of faith and spiritual discovery.

Prayer is an act of faith and relationship. It begins with the faith that God is there to receive prayer, otherwise why pray at all? Just as we do not completely understand the intense loves we have, we still act upon them faithfully and even sacrificially. So even though we do not understand God and prayer, we experience the power of both when we include them in our daily lives.

What do we do before we ask for something specific? My answer is to think about it carefully, see if it seems appropriate and important to our lives. Tony Campolo wrote that he believes that sometimes miracles are performed through prayer when they are absolutely essential to save a person's faith.

He tells a story about when he was thirteen and his family had entered some very tough financial times. He was trying to be a really good kid and help out his family while in his junior year in high school. He held down a couple of jobs while attending school and one of those jobs involved making deliveries for a pharmacy on his bicycle. One very cold, rainy night he had just finished his deliveries at nearly midnight and was riding his bicycle home, when his front tire blew out.

He wrote,

"I had worked so hard making deliveries to earn a few extra dollars to help my mother pay our bills. I had done everything I knew how to do to be a good boy, and I was worn out and tired beyond anyone's imagination. So when the tire blew out, I just sat down on the curb of the street and cried. I remember saying, 'God: Everybody thinks you are good and kind. But if you really were good and kind, this would not be happening. I would not be out here stranded on this cold miserable night. You would help me.'"

Eventually he pushed his disabled bike toward home, weeping in frustration, freezing cold, and absolute misery. After less than a block he came upon a gas station and even though he was sure that the pumps were turned off, and that his tire wouldn't hold air anyway he hooked up a nozzle to his tire. He was wrong on both counts. The air did stream out of the hose and his bike tire did hold air.

He got onto his bike and rode home. After he arrived home he lifted his bike onto the front porch and then as he put the key in the lock of the front door he heard it. A loud hissing sound announced that the air in the blown tire had just completely disappeared.

"Perhaps" he writes, "that miracle was the only thing that could have saved an exhausted, sad teenager from being lost to the Kingdom of God."

So what is prayer?

Prayer is the conversation with God, which changes us. It is the dialogue with the ultimate source of life and meaning over the ultimate matters of our lives. It is the way that we seek insight, strength and spiritual wisdom. It is a way that we strengthen our perseverance. It is seeking a conversation with God to acquire the personal qualities which brings us the peace which passes understanding, and extends it into the world around us.

Prayer is sharing with God not only our deepest joys and needs; but also the deepest joys and needs of others and the world around us. It is one of those ultimate acts of admission that we are connected to other people and events besides those directly touching our being. In our seeking the welfare of the world in prayer, we fundamentally grow in our connection to the world and its needs.

If you want to know what prayer is really like, then try it. Nothing is gained by just discussing it. If you want to further your prayer life, then pray more often, more honestly, and with greater depth. Jesus said that what we seek in prayer we will find.

What we find is that we are found by God, and that always means some wonderful, but surprising changes.

May your prayer life be fruitful and abundant.

Asking the Hard Questions

April 3, 2005

I was once put in the position of being seen by a group of passionate Christians as a "Doubting Thomas." It was the year my brother and I were moved from the San Fernando Valley and away from our foster parents to live with our real mother in Alhambra, California. It was not an easy transition. It was not something that either of us wanted, but we had to accept it. As usual my brother and I clung to one another, forging a bond of protection.

We sought some solace in a new Christian community and signed up for Vacation Bible School at the local Baptist Church. I was in a large class of sixth graders headed for junior high in September, and I spent a couple of weeks singing Baptist songs, learning Bible stories about the love of Jesus and the need to believe that He died for my sins. But for me this was nothing new. I had a foster sister whose love and caring for her little foster brother had convinced me that Jesus of Nazareth would be the expression of God in my life, and that if I let him into my heart, as she told me, I would never need to fear death or abandonment by people. You see, foster kids feared abandonment more than death and hell.

I ultimately relished the warm, loving presence of grown-ups who made me feel as if Jesus was walking beside me, helping me deal with the life I hadn't chosen. t also gave me a chance to feel out this new world, hopefully in a place that would not damage my emotional fabric as the recent move had done.

It was the last day of Bible school and, as expected, the final altar call was made. I wondered how many of my large class really needed to make the decision I had made three years earlier with my loving foster sister as my guide. As the piano played softly in the background the trio of adult Vacation Church teachers emotionally invited students to come forward and choose to let Jesus into their hearts.

I could feel the gravity of the teachers' entreaties to make a commitment to Christ. It was certainly creating and forcing up a tide of response, even in me. I thought to myself, *to go forward to the altar would be to lie, to say I was not a believer when I already was.* If I got up, the teachers would give me a look of approval and acceptance. But was that what I was supposed to do? Go forward to win their approval, make their day?

That's when I became "Doubting Thomas." I started to wonder, would kids go up just because they liked these teachers and didn't want to disappoint them, or seem to be challenging their wisdom? Would kids go forward just because their good friend did, or they felt disloyal or socially pressured? Would anyone check this out, or care? This made me uncomfortable. I knew I had nothing more to offer up than what I had offered when I had decided to be a follower of Jesus like my foster sister. So I had no need to go forward.

I began to have nagging doubts about this process, wondering how anyone would test the real motives of those who would be drawn forward by the invitation. I noticed over half the class was standing. The invitation seemed to grow stronger, and the social pressure increased. It wasn't long before everyone in the class was standing in the saved line, while one student sat refusing to join them. Me.

I suppose one of the things that motivated me was what had happened to me that summer. My whole life had been turned upside down and I had no choice in what would happen to me. Here was a situation where I was again being told by well meaning adults to do what they needed me to do for my own good. There was no reason I could think of for me to accommodate them. I had used up my desire to just make adults happy when I entered the social worker's car willingly and didn't cry and scream, and hold onto the gate posts.

As I sat there I was asked if I didn't want to just come forward and recommit my life to Jesus, as if it weren't good enough when I came in the door that morning. It took all of my will power to say it, but I said, "I don't need to recommit. I'm already a Christian."

There was silence from my peers as the teachers quietly murmured about what to do with the one hold out, the "Doubting Thomas." In that moment I came to understand Thomas, and to truly appreciate what Jesus did for him. Unlike Jesus, no one there thought my doubts were worthy of being addressed.

Years after my experience of being Thomas in the eyes of my Vacation Church School teachers and classmates, I thought about what Jesus would have done had he made the invitation. I think Jesus would have wondered about who I was. I think Jesus would have told me it was a good thing that I was saying what I really felt. And he would not have left me alone, but he would have sat down and gotten to know me, found out about the upheaval in my life, seen the hurt in my eyes, realized how silly it was to try to get me to say something I thought untrue. He would have seen how I wanted to start feeling connected to something again and he would have said, "Hey Billy, would you mind being with me while I talk to the other kids who want to believe in me?

Sure, I know some of them just wanted to make the teachers happy, but maybe you could help them be honest."

I would have answered, "Yes, Jesus." And in my heart I would have said, "When I grow up I want to be just like YOU."

Choosing to See

March 10, 2002

When I was a young minister working at First United
Presbyterian Church in San Francisco, I was driving to work
one day on Sunset Boulevard, a divided road which ran from
Golden Gate park due South. When I approached the left
turn I made each time I went to work, I noticed a policeman
on a large horse crossing the road ahead of me. I carefully
slowed and stopped, my blinker signaling my intention to
turn left. The policeman began staring at me as he crossed
ahead of me and turned all the way around in his saddle as he
crossed the street, watching me closely as I made the left
turn. Ever so deliberately the policeman on the handsome
chestnut horse extended his arm and waved me over for a
talk.

I was truly puzzled by the policeman's action. Something
about me obviously disturbed him. He leaned down from the
saddle and said incredulously, "Didn't you see that sign?" I
said, "What sign?" He pointed at a prominently displayed "no
left turn" sign that had been directly in my line of vision as I
made the left turn. I starred at it in disbelief. It hadn't been
there yesterday, or the day before. I was certain of that. Or
had it?

The police officer could see my confusion. He said, "The
traffic sign is new, but you really didn't see it?" I stared at
him, dumbfounded. How could I have missed such a big

sign? I replied, "I make this turn every day and I haven't ever seen that sign until you pointed it out."

It was obvious to the policeman that my familiarity had completely blinded me to the new sign, even when it was right in front of my nose. Mercifully he let me go, telling me to remember not to make the turn again. It was a good lesson on how one can see something, and because of a presupposition, not "see" it at all.

We have a choice in our spiritual lives as well: the choice to see. It is the choice to see the world and ourselves as God sees it and us. It is the choice to face the many ways in which we blind ourselves to God's truth about ourselves, others, and events in our lives.

In his immortal hymn, *Amazing Grace*, John Newton wrote "I once was lost, but now am found, was blind but now I see." What he wrote about was the terrible life he had led before he had discovered the loving and compassionate reality of the grace of God. This life had been an almost intentional self blinding of his soul to a living relationship with God.

Born in London in 1725, John Newton spent the early years of his life in the loving care of his mother while his father earned a living at sea. Her guidance of his religious life was effective as far as it went, but she died when Newton was 7 years old. After that the religious training ceased. As a result of his father's trade as a ship's captain, Newton became a seafarer at a very young age and experienced a life of wild dissipation so often characteristic of the men of that arduous and dangerous trade during the 18th century. History tells us, John Newton became a vile, divisive, and abusive young man. He betrayed people who treated him with kindness and respect. Surely, he suffered for his cruelties, and experienced periods of remorse and repentance, but then he would relapse into even more vile, destructive and cruel behavior. He rejected the faith he had learned as a child as he ridiculed and made fun of believers, and did many cruel acts to show contempt for the ethical and moral sensitivities of honest people of faith.

But after surviving a great and tragic storm while serving aboard a British *Man-of-War*, Newton was stripped of his contemptuous pride and became uncharacteristically reflective about the direction of his life. As a result he renewed the Christian faith taught him by his beloved mother. Yet it did not prevent him from becoming the master of a slave ship. He believed at first that his faith required him to only treat slaves fairly and humanely.

Newton eventually left seafaring life, married a young woman he had loved for many years, and became a well known and beloved clergyman. His wife's unfaltering love, and the realization that God could accept and forgive someone who had done such terrible things as he had done, opened Newton's eyes to a whole new world of happiness and hope. It particularly opened his eyes to the reality that the slaves he had once seen as inferior and deserving of their servitude, were in the eyes of God humans of equal worth, capable of the same grace that had accepted him into the kingdom of God. Newton's preaching and writing were part of the influences that turned around the thinking of England, so that shortly before his death, England abolished the slave trade forever.

The grace of God gives people a new vision, a new look at life. Paul had once looked upon all Gentiles as unclean infidels, people to be avoided. He regarded the followers of Christ as lower than Gentiles because they were blasphemers of the dogma of his faith. As blasphemers, even the death penalty was not too great a punishment. But, after being blinded on the road to Damascus by a vision of the risen

Christ, and healed by the gentle ministrations of a Christian named Ananias, Paul opened his eyes anew to the world. Suddenly what had seemed so righteous to Paul, now only looked cruel, egotistical and dark. He obviously wondered at the fact that God would readily forgive him and accept him, after all of the suffering he had brought to others.

We can use that *Amazing Grace* too. We can use it when we are blind to truths about ourselves, and don't want to look at them because we find them too painful to admit. While watching the Super Bowl on television, I was astounded to see a glitzy rock star strutting across an improvised stage about to croon away about the American experience of 9-11. I had a certain impression of rock stars. I believed they were all shallow individuals, motivated by their egocentrism and prone to sing about injustices in the world and risk nothing to personally involve them in setting them straight.

Later, I ran across a magazine article about an unusual rock star named, Bono. To my surprise Bono was the rock star I had seen during the Super Bowl performance; the rock star I had so righteously criticized for shallowness and hypocrisy. The article describes how he and his wife were shocked by the death and poverty they experienced on a tour of Africa. Instead of recoiling from it and retreating to the life of glamour and excess, they sought to comprehend what was happening by venturing out into the turmoil of famine and squalor. This galvanized Bono to do something other than just sing about it. So he educated himself about the issues facing poor countries and became involved in leading world efforts in dealing with Third World Debt and hunger and disease in Africa. I was most impressed with his words at the end of the article when he contrasts singing with his group, "U2" and working in the tough area of world deprivation and want. He says,

"When you sing, you make people vulnerable to change in their lives. You make yourself vulnerable to change in your life. But in the end, you've got to become the change you want to see in the world. I'm actually not a very good example of that -- I'm too selfish, and the right to be ridiculous is something I hold too dear- but still, I know it's true."

Interestingly, though Bono in his honesty criticizes his own shortcomings in becoming the change he wants in the world, yet his tireless efforts, flawed as they might be, testify to the great good that can come when one does as he has done, and becomes the change he wants to make in the world.

I must admit that in reading about Bono I had to honestly face a blindness I also had. I was one to quickly discount any good that could come from someone who strutted around a stage, who appeared so egotistically self-absorbed in public, and who swallowed a microphone during performances. In short, I was faced with the prejudices and presuppositions that cut me off from the honest, effort of another human being to understand how God's compassion can and should be manifested in the world. Now, I only wish that some of the stars of the classical stage I so admire, who perform the music which inspires my own pilgrimage and search for the sound of God passing in my life, would have the same clarity of vision as Bono.

This experience has made me sit back and think about my own spiritual blindness. I wonder what else I am missing of God in other people and other events because of my judgments, my unexamined habits and my assumptions. Was I acting like the temple officers, who couldn't see the great act of healing for what it was because they were fixed upon their vexation about an insignificant breach of ritual habit?

The grace of God is the assurance that we need have no fear of looking squarely at ourselves and dealing with even the most foolish, clown-like aspects of what we find there. In the end God isn't interested in what is so terrible about us, but in working with what is redeeming about us. It does no good to look into ourselves for what is redeeming about someone we admire. To accept God's grace, we ourselves must be willing to accept what is redeeming about us.

I could live all of my life in peace because though I know God accepts me, even with my lack of talent for dealing with great detail. I am still searching in my personality for the place where I store the ability for sorting out details like the accountant I value so much. In the end, I will have to understand that God is willing to make a pretty wonderful life out of my shortcoming with detail sorting, if I am willing to let God do this.

Jesus once said, don't worry about the sliver that has gotten in the eye of your neighbor and obstructed his vision. He said to worry instead about the block of wood stuck in your own eye that prevents you from seeing your neighbor at all. He assured his listeners that if they allowed the grace of God to remove the obstructions from their vision, God would help them deal with the truth of the world they would see.

The grace and compassion of God is assured to us by Christ. It is the agent which allows us to spiritually see. It will cure spiritual blindness. But first you must ask yourself, "Do I really want to see?"

Do you?

As John Newton wrote, "I once was lost, but now am found, was blind but now I see!"

Night Vision Goggles

March 26, 2006

When I was a child, my foster parents used to take the family camping. When the lantern was put out, I was truly amazed at how completely dark it was. I couldn't even see my hand in front of my face. But as my eyes became adjusted to the dark, I became aware of a glow coming from the outside. It was starlight shining in from the darkness through the mosquito netting. Night vision goggles build on the reality that even on the darkest night, there is light glowing all around us. These devices take in the light unseen by our natural vision. They take in light that comes from the glow in a cloudy sky, the lights from distant cities and from the stars. Night vision goggles amplify these faint signals of light and boost them to the visible range.

To be born anew according to John is to live in awareness of the light. The light is God's light, glowing in all that is about us, and even inside of us.

Jesus is saying here in John that faithful awareness of God's love is like night vision goggles. It makes us able to see the light of goodness and harmony shining through the reality of the darkness. However, we must choose to nourish the light in us and use it in our daily walk.

When we believe what Jesus has said about the nature of God, ourselves and the world, we can turn on this vision with patient and compassionate perception. It is then that everything glows with a shape and form, and the spirit of Christ illumines what was dimly seen and barely revealed.

When I was recovering from my second heart attack, I was lying in the ICU unit at Diablo Hospital dealing with constant pain. The pain had settled in my back, and I frequently wanted to move to seek some kind of comfort. But the medical procedures required that I lay completely still. In order to relax, I meditated, and did so for hours, using all the discipline I had learned over the years of placing myself outside of myself and in the hands of the eternal.

During all of this pain and immobility, I remember looking around at all of the equipment, the sick people in the unit, and the nurses and technicians. In the midst of all of that there seemed to be a glow. It's difficult to explain, but it seemed as if everything glowed with benevolent meaning and peace.

When my friends came to visit and pray for me, they stood over my bed looking so serious. I wanted to tell them that everything was glowing with a quiet calm, and whatever the outcome, it all made sense and was part of God's plan.

It turns out that the glowing experience was one of the moments in my life when all of the indicators said I was the closest to dying and my friends feared that it was imminent. But even in the shadow of death there is the warmest of light that we can access with prayer, meditation and other spiritual disciplines.

The light isn't there just in moments of surrender to life threatening illness. It is always there. It is most important to look for it in the hustle and bustle of daily life. When the light of God's love, compassion, mercy and wisdom is brought forth to transform the dark landscape of our daily living, things become clearer and harmonious in our lives.

Night vision is spiritual vision. When we view people with patient, sincere interest, we are using our night vision. We are able to compassionately accept what we find, knowing it to be part of what makes up the human condition. Sometimes this requires us to help, offer guidance, information, and advice. Other times it calls for the need to be quiet and just be present, allowing the other person to reveal what is on their mind and heart. Sometimes it calls forth straight talk, and merciful disagreement. Other times it means to be patient and wait. Spiritual night vision means putting aside decorum, social expectations and being in the light of the moment.

The Reverend Fred Craddock told me several stories of how his view of a certain situation was shadowed by his judgment and sense of social custom. He was conducting a funeral in Bluefield, West Virginia for a 17-year-old boy who had been killed in a car accident. He said,

"As it turned out, he was one of eleven children. The other ten, healthy and capable surrounded their mother, who was a widow. She screamed out several times at the church funeral and then twice again at the cemetery: 'If I had known this was going to happen, I would never have had any children.'

I looked at the ten children staring at their mother and listening to her outbursts. It bothered me, so I got them together and I said, 'Now, your mother is very distraught. She doesn't really mean what she is saying.'

One of older children said to me, 'Yes she does. But if I were the one who was killed, she would've said it too."

Spiritual goggles help us not to jump to conclusions, but to let the facts emerge on their own, in their own time.

In a little church in which Reverend Craddock was a guest preacher, he was invited by a lady to have lunch at her home. She was a widow and was alone. He wrote.

"We went into the house, and she said, 'Go into the den and read the paper and watch TV. I'll have lunch ready in a minute.' She put on her apron, and went into the dining room to set places for lunch. I followed her to the dining room and said, 'Now, don't go to all this trouble for me. I eat in the kitchen at home.'

She ignored me and pulled out a drawer and took out a linen tablecloth and linen napkins. She put the cloth on, the napkins on, and then took out beautiful stemmed glasses. She wiped the dust out and I said again, 'We eat in the kitchen at home.' She seemed not to hear me and went right on with the table setting. I said, a little louder this time, 'Look, I mean it's just the two of us. We eat in the kitchen at home.'

She turned around and with a level gaze said to me, 'Will you be quiet and sit down?'

I said, a little sheepishly, 'Well, I suppose I will.'

She looked over at me and asked, 'Do you have any idea what it's like fixing a meal for one?'

And so we ate in the dining room with beautiful stemmed glasses, candles and her finest linens."

The message here is to turn away from the dark terrain of your judgment, expectations, agendas, disappointments and hurts. Allow people, things, events, and life itself, to glow with the spirit that is apart from you. Gaze through the night vision goggles of God's loving grace, and rejoice.

To Speak for the Wind

June 3, 2001

In 1952, a bridge was built over the Tacoma Narrows in Puget Sound, Washington. It was a beautiful bridge and deemed structurally sturdy, but only four months after it was opened the bridge collapsed and fell into the Sound.

In news photos of the event, the bridge begins to swing, almost undetectably, then the roadway begins to heave, and within moments the whole bridge is writhing back and forth, up and down, twisting and turning, until a few of the giant cables give way, and the bridge plunges into the water.

On that particular day, the wind velocity was considered moderate but combined with the direction of the wind, the suspension cables began to vibrate and hum. It was somewhat like the strings of a piano in a harmonic arrangement; when one string begins to hum, others join in and soon all of the strings/cables are vibrating, setting up the violent reaction.

At the time, the engineers and architects who had designed the bridge didn't know about this particular harmonic principle. They studied the plans over and over and tested their concepts and designs, but could find nothing wrong with them. Finally, it was determined that the bridge failure must have been due to sloppy workmanship or faulty materials. They decided to rebuild the bridge just as it had been before.

A Hungarian born physicist, Theodore von Karman, heard about it and went to the architects and said to them, "If you rebuild it just the same way it was before, it will fall down again, just the same as it did before." He understood the harmonic principle involved, which has since been named in textbooks, 'Von Karman's Vortex.'

The architects and engineers were not pleased at being questioned by this unknown outsider and were disturbed at being accused of causing the problem. They thought perhaps von Karman was working for someone else in the industry, or representing an outside interest. They began to harshly question him, asking, "Whom do you work for? What is your interest in this? Whom do you speak for?"

Von Karman looked directly at them, and answered in his elegant Hungarian accent, "I speak for the wind."

To the ancient Hebrews, the wind was the movement of one of the basic elements in the universe. In the Greek influenced world in which they lived, all things were made of earth, fire, water or air. When they described the Spirit of God, which enlivens all things, they used the word "ruach" meaning the wind of God. This divine wind was the power of God which when breathed into the nostrils of a human, gave it life. And when it was withdrawn, it brought death. Ruach is the word we translate as Spirit of God or Holy Spirit.

The Holy Spirit, this creating consciousness, was the spirit that filled Mary with the courage to be the mother of Jesus. This was the spirit that gave Moses the ability to appear before Pharaoh, with no power save his staff and his belief in the righteous God of the Universe. This spirit moved Moses to demand that Pharaoh, the most powerful potentate on earth, release a band of slaves from his possession. This was the spirit that gave Jesus the ability to face the crucifixion without wavering. It was the power that raised Him and caused His astounded, traumatized followers to renew their hope in the Divine Jesus. This was the spirit, which energized Peter to address a crowd of his countrymen and convince thousands of them to follow the leading of Jesus to a life of grace, forgiveness and restoration.

When Von Karman spoke for the wind, he spoke for a physical force that simply had to be reckoned with to prevent another disaster. When the New Testament speaks for the Holy Spirit, it speaks for the principle of God's loving will, which must be reckoned with or human life and enterprise will fail.

The work of the Holy Spirit is not just personal, although we often speak of the Holy Spirit in terms of how humans experience its presence in their personal lives. The Holy Spirit bears the intentions of God for our universe and all dimensions of existence.

The work of the Holy Spirit is apparent each time a supernova sprays heavy metals light years into space, or when a galaxy merges into another galaxy, increasing the possibilities of new life and a new consciousness in our universe.

The Holy Spirit is not just a physical force behind what appears to be the randomness in our physics. The Holy Spirit is personal and conscious as well as powerful. It resonates with the consciousness of God and must be considered when we seek to know the meaning of our lives and make conscious choices about our lives. When we are out of step with it, like the bridge over the Sound, our cables sing with the warning hum of building tension, and sooner or later our enterprises collapse.

The Bible speaks for the wind, the spirit of God. It speaks of those things that humans need to do with their lives, which take account of the intentions of God. The witness of the Bible calls to believers of all ages to likewise speak for the wind. We must speak for the wind by living lives, which bear the presence of God's loving spirit. God commands us to do four basic things in response to the Holy Spirit:

1. That we love God, our neighbor and ourselves.
2. That we live justly.
3. That we act compassionately with each other.
4. That we construct wholesome communities where we can pool our wisdom and increase the power of our insight.

Let me say something about each of these four basic responses:

1. To love God will never mean that we possess God. God possesses us. We love God because we experience the awesome wonder of the spirit alive in creation, loving us and all things. Loving God is an active verb. It is not a static state of mind. To love God is to grow in God's love for ourselves and our neighbor.

2. Secondly, to speak for the wind, to respond to the Holy Spirit is to know that the Spirit is about justice. Micah 6:8 says that it is required that we do justly, love tenderly, and walk humbly before the Lord our God. Seeking to live justly is not an optional response to the Holy Spirit; it is a required response, one which will naturally occur to anyone who is earnest about letting God into one's life.

3. Third, to speak for the wind, we should live compassionately, so our lives do not resist the spirit's harmony. This is more than being nice. This means living in the spirit of the Good Samaritan who humbly, and without thought of reward, bound up the wounded traveler and sacrificed his time and money so that healing could be

achieved.

4. Finally, living in resonance, instead of resistance to the spirit is living in a way which enhances community. This advances the healthy means in which humans can multiply the effect of their caring work by acting together instead of singly. Community is always hard to establish, difficult to keep going in a creative direction, and bothersome to nurture. But it is only in an assembly that we reach our deepest understandings of the nature of God. And it will be in groups that we formulate the directions that lead us through the great challenges put before us. In this way we are nurtured toward wisdom.

Washington Irving once wrote, "There is in every heart a spark of heavenly fire which lies dormant in the broad daylight of prosperity, but which kindles up and beams and blazes in the dark hour of adversity." Then, he might say, it is also there to speak for the wind of God.

When Liver Tastes Like Steak

Easter, 2001

When I was a young lad living with foster parents, my foster mother was a fine cook, but very fundamental in her approach to cooking; she used very few spices and embellishments in the dishes she prepared for the family. We ate well, and we ate heartily. But we ate plainly.

I loved my foster mother's baked chicken, and ham, and corn on the cob with biscuits and gravy. But there were two things she insisted on cooking from time to time, which was the bane of my existence: liver and okra. To my palate, liver tasted like softened tin cans. Even the texture seemed to suggest what that organ had been doing inside a cow in the first place. There were some things a young kid like me just didn't want to know about the food placed in front of him.

Okra presented another problem. When I was in the second grade I read about the Yang Na Indians of the Los Angeles basin. They were a peaceful hunter-gatherer tribe on the coast of California who built dwellings called *wikiups* and collected acorns to grind for food. Intrigued by this idea, I once tried to sup on a handful of acorns. It proved to be a very bad idea. So whenever I was served okra, I was immediately reminded of those bitter acorns I had tried to eat like the Yang Na Indians.

I dreaded mealtimes when I knew liver or okra was on the menu. I used to think that the true end of my dining experience would arrive the night when my foster mom would try to serve both at the same meal. Mercifully, this never happened.

In the summer after my graduation from the 6th grade, my brother and I left our foster home and moved in with our real mother. My mother's cooking was different from what we had been used to, because my mother cooked with a certain Latin flair. She liked to use plenty of spices and seasonings that made the food interesting and tasty.

One day my brother and I walked into the kitchen and found, next to the stove, a quivering, threatening hunk of liver. We could feel our taste buds recede and disappear at the memory of the dreaded organ meat. My mother sensed our pain; not a difficult thing to do since my brother was making retching noises while holding his hand over his mouth.

She smiled at us and asked how we could be so sure that we wouldn't like what she was cooking, since she had never prepared liver for us before. Jack and I looked at each other incredulously. How could anyone say such a thing about liver? Why would anyone want to serve a piece of meat which had no bones, trembled while waiting to be consumed, and tasted like cat food gone bad.

"Liver makes me want to barf before I even get it into my mouth," my brother said. He was never one for subtlety.

She looked at both of us patiently and said, "Well, just try it the way I make it."

We waited gloomily for the cooking to finish and the serving to begin. When the dish arrived at the table, the liver seemed to look and smell differently than I had remembered. The meat platter was adorned with garnish and onions and almost looked presentable. My brother and I gingerly cut into our portions and took several small bites. It seemed to taste a bit like a juicy steak. Transformed by my mom's knowledge of herbs and spices, the much-maligned organ has become a delicious and tasty meal for her discerning young sons.

A few days later the same thing happened with okra. It showed up buried in a magnificent cheese casserole which altered the bitter acorn-tasting vegetable into something that tasted like macaroni. It was amazing what my mom could do with sauces and herbs and spices to bring both health and delight to the dinner table each evening.

If all of life was as pleasant as steak and macaroni was to my young palate, there would be no cause to celebrate the resurrection. We would have experienced no tragedies or pain or confusion, or no death. We would either live forever, as happy little quantum of consciousness, or we would be gathered into heaven with an ability to communicate between this life and the next so we would never have to really be apart.

The reason we celebrate the resurrection is that a large part of life is liver and okra that we are trying to make taste like steak and macaroni. Along with life's many joys we also face disappointments, pain, fears, deterioration, and most of all death. In Shakespeare's play, *Macbeth*, his protagonist surveys all of the fear and agony, the evil and darkness invading his life and concludes that all of life is nothing more than liver and okra, and nothing seemed to make it taste better.

Macbeth sorrowfully declares, "Life is a poor player who struts and frets his hour upon the stage and then is heard no more. It is a tale told by an idiot, full of sound and fury, signifying nothing."

On the first day of the week after Jesus' execution, the two Marys, Joanna, and other women went to his tomb, trying to assuage the pain in their hearts caused by his loss. For them and for the disciples, life had become a poorly prepared meal of liver and okra. The powerful had won. The promised light of the world that had filled their common lives with vision and purpose seemed to have been extinguished.

Much had been lost with the death of Jesus and they were filled with loss and despair. Jesus had given his people the light of eternal hope and had made their lives significant. The light of Christ made each follower appear to be connected to a profound, everlasting totality, and shine with worth and meaning. Choosing to live the kind of loving, merciful and forgiving life Jesus lived became possible when one believed that all of life was interwoven in a divine purpose. The way Jesus taught, and more importantly, the way he lived, convinced those around him of the reality of that interwoven, driving purpose and of a secure place in that purpose for each person.

When the grieving women went to the tomb and found it empty, and filled with the light of angels proclaiming the resurrection they saw again the light of that divine purpose stream into their lives. It illuminated the darkness, turned their pains and disappointments into hope.

All of the things that had tasted like liver and okra began to take on the flavor of steak and macaroni. The rising of Jesus from the dead signified his power to turn the okra and liver events of life into macaroni and steak. It was real; and it remains real.

The resurrection is the power that allows us to view all of the events of life as a great and wonderful meal, even though we encounter issues that remind us of liver and okra.

Henri Nouwen, a writer and priest who died in 1996, wrote the book called **Can You Drink the Cup**. The book was a short commentary on the lessons he learned after 10 years working at L' Arche Community in Toronto, Canada, a home for people with serious mental disabilities. The community contained people who were completely paralyzed, but with bright intellects and who were always struggling to find ways to express their feelings and thoughts; others, who were not only mentally disabled but also regularly battered by inner voices that they could not control; still others, who suffered from muscular dystrophy, and who required breathing machines and who were in constant fear of falling. The list went on and on.

Nouwen discovered that these people were often able to assess their lives, with all of their tragedies and losses, and claim their disability as a joyous experience of God's love and grace. They believed, as Jesus said, their lives were part of a greater whole. This heartfelt belief was what could turn liver to steak and okra to macaroni for them each day.

Given the message of Nouwen's book, he is saying to us that we can make steak out of liver if we look at our lives through the grace, mercy and love which Christ showed us in his death and resurrection.

In John, Jesus says, "I am the light of the world. Whoever follows me will never walk in darkness but will have the light of life." And when challenged on this statement by religious authorities Jesus said, "Even if I testify on my own behalf, my testimony is valid because I know where I have come from and where I am going, but you do not know where I come from or where I am going. You judge by human standards; I judge no one."

Jesus asks everyone to examine his or her life in the light of the resurrection. He bids all of us to boldly, and honestly gaze anew at all of the moving parts of which we are; and see the whole of our lives through the lenses of God's love and purpose. If you look, don't judge and become defensive or blinded by false pride. Look with the eyes of God, the perspective of the place from whence your soul really came, the place to where it is going.

We are born of heaven, and we return to that place, the place of deepest knowledge, and profoundest wisdom and beauty. We are here to add to our growing store of that knowledge and wisdom, to contribute to the unfolding of the kingdom of heaven. It is our mission to apply the knowledge of the resurrection to the joys and pathos of life.

Faith in Christ's victory over death gives us the way to view our lives as meaningful gifts of God which include the terrible parts of our lives as well as the magnificent components. Faith is the spice that can turn our liver and okra to steak and macaroni.

Life as a gift has intrinsic Spiritual meaning. We are created to engage that meaning, not avoid it. And the only way to truly engage it is to do so with faith that God is truly in control and has intended for our lives to count.

What is left to us is to employ this faith. We are blest with the capacity to love, though we know every wonderful and life-fulfilling love may also result in loss and mourning. There is no other way to experience the fullness of love than to risk both its gains and losses.

The resurrection invites us to boldly embrace life as God's gift, unafraid of failing. In God's eyes there is no failure or loss for those who embrace the life he has given to them, and live it graciously and mercifully.

The gracious love of Jesus Christ can and does turn the tastes of life's liver and okra to steak and macaroni.

The cowboy outfits were made by our beloved foster grandmother. She lived in Kansas where she made seat covers. The vests and chaps were made from seat cover material. She also made the hats. We loved these outfits!

Choosing Not to Be Small about Faith

March 26, 2000

When I was a boy, living in a foster home with my brother, we considered ourselves the lucky ones. We shared the home with a younger foster brother and sister, David and Donna and it felt like a real family. Our foster mother was a good and thrifty daughter of Kansas farmers, who always had our best interests at heart. We liked to believe that is why she decided one day that we needed to eat whole grain cereal for breakfast. Not only was it nutritious, she reasoned, but it was inexpensive too. She bought some right-out-of-the-field grain which she may have soaked in water for a day or two and then after drying it, served it to us for breakfast.

It was terrible!! It was worse than liver. No matter how much sugar any of us put on it, the stuff tasted like sun-dried lawn clippings. Our instant reactions met with stolid discipline from my mom. "Just eat it and don't complain," she said. "You're lucky to have food on your table." It was the same mantra that made virtues of all of the insufferable foods from lima beans to okra.

When my mom left the room my brother and I began to eat our cereal while softly uttering the sounds of selected barnyard animals. My brother mooed and I bleated softly like a sheep or goat. As we did the sound effects, we kept our eyes peeled and ears attentive to our mom's return. Before long we had inspired our little foster brother, then about five, to join us. David, a rebellious sort even at his tender age, was always quick to join our revolts. We always managed to make sure he never knew when the game was over and the revolt needed to turn into meek capitulation.

When mom returned, David was grunting like a pig and rooting around in his mushy gruel. My brother looked at him critically and said something like, "David, you're making me sick." Of course this only spurred him on, so I said, "You better eat instead of play with that or you'll never finish it."

The results were predictable. David, who didn't like being bossed around by his older siblings, made more obnoxious noises, which caused our foster mom to demand that he eat every kernel of his cereal. A scene ensued with David refusing and mom demanding; it finally ended when David was made to eat all his food and sit quietly on his stool for another 15 minutes. Somehow, this seemed to make an impression on my mom. It was the last time we saw this experiment in "back to the soil" nutrition

I remember going to Sunday school not long after that incident and hearing the story of Cain and Abel. The teacher read to us how Cain brought God cereal from his farming, while his brother brought God lamb chops and lamb stew. The teacher said, "God did not like Cain's sacrifice." Instantly, I knew why. Cain had brought God the same cereal my mom had tried to serve us. God must have known it was worse than a helping of liver served on a bed of lima beans. For years this was my interpretation of why Cain got into trouble with God.

Of course I was wrong. The Hebrew holy men had written about this matter long before Jesus knotted a rope and let the money changers in the Temple courtyard know of his attitude concerning their commercial enterprise. Cain's problem was not what he brought, but the spirit in which he brought it. Cain brought his gift, but he didn't present himself. Certainly, he had dispensed with his obligation, but he had not come seeking an encounter with God, a relationship that would change and shape his own life. Biblical history tells us that sacrifices of the Old Testament were never supposed to be automatic, ritualistic events. Instead, it was to be an experience that brought a revelation of the gravity of what it meant to have a sincere desire to put God first in life.

According to the Gospel of John, after Jesus had performed the miracle of changing water into wine at the marriage in Cana, he and his mother, disciples, and brothers, went to Capernaum, and then on to Jerusalem to celebrate the Passover. It was a season of serious recommitment; sacrifices were central to the rites which had traditionally accompanied that recommitment.

Sacrifice was an important component of the life of faith in the culture of Jesus' time. Sacrifice revealed the depth of one's sincerity. It showed that one put God's will above one's own needs. The Law of Moses stated what kinds of sacrifices should be made at the temple. Animals were killed in the temple and either parts of the animal or the whole animal were offered up to God. Unused parts of the animals were given to the priests to feed them and to provide resources for the poor and needy of the community.

Often religious duty required that one bring to the temple a young male sheep, or a kid, or a pair of pigeons for sacrifice by the priests for the worshiper. In the old rural days this was easy to do. People had sheep or goats or pigeons right at home from which to select their sacrifice. But in Jesus' day, as in ours, city people didn't keep those kinds of animals hanging around the apartment. So when a city worshipper went to the temple to make a sacrifice, the temple authorities arranged to have sacrificial animals for sale on the premises. The only catch was that you had to use temple coins to make the purchase. If you didn't have temple currency available to make the purchase, you could change your Roman money into temple money in the temple's outer courtyard.

Of course with Passover bringing thousands of worshippers to the temple, the trade was brisk. And it was the custom to charge premium prices for the money changing and for the animals. All one has to do is visit the floor of the stock exchange or see the traders in futures at the Chicago exchange to visualize what happened in the courtyard of the temple. The gospel tells us Jesus walked into this environment, this up-to-date full-service temple, and saw the people selling the cattle and the sheep and the birds. He saw the money-changers at their counters with their constantly changing rates of exchange. He heard the noise, the shouting, the bargaining, the bragging, the bleating and the cooing, and he smelled the sweat and the dung of the nervous animals. He saw and heard and smelled all these things that were being sold for the salvation of God's people and he became exceedingly angry.

Jesus took a cord, probably his belt, and lashed out with it, flailing at the merchants and the moneychangers, tossing over their tables and flinging their coins to the ground. He opened the cages and set the birds free. He ran about, chasing the cattle and sheep and their owners from the courtyard, all the while shouting, "Stop this! What have you done? Get these things out of here! You have turned my father's house into a market place instead of a house of prayer. You've made it a den of thieves. Get out, Get out!"

The point of bringing God a sacrifice was to enter into the process of weighing the worth of things and into that formula considering the worth of the love of God. When the sacrifice was made, the individual was to be in a state of contemplation of the meaning of the worth of God's love of him or her, and God's grace in giving and sustaining life. This was the moment when the worshipper made his serious vows or his promises to God.

The gospel of John begins by telling us that the very core of the purposes of being was contained in the witness of Jesus of Nazareth. "In the beginning was the Word, and the word was with God and the Word was God. and the Word became Flesh, and dwelt among us full of grace and truth." No wonder then, that John says that the first revelation of Jesus' purpose on earth was taken so seriously by the people he confronted with his message, that they left their very livelihoods to follow him.

During Lent, we contemplate the choices of faith. The stories of Cain and of Jesus' frustration with the moneychangers present us with that same choice. We need to choose to be big about our faith, and not small.

This means a myriad of things to different people. I had an example of it recently when I watched a group of bike riders fill up one whole lane of a major thoroughfare in the city. It seemed to me that being in a pack of bikers, decked out in expensive biking gear and enjoying state of the art bikes, seemed to give these riders a false belief in their entitlement to hold-up car traffic. I found myself wanting to honk the horn and yell at them to ride single file at the side of the road like I had been taught by my foster mom.

My wife could see that my muttering was only stoking the fires of high blood pressure and said so. In that instant I realized how I was letting this insignificant violation of human rules color my view of the world at that moment. Would God see these people this way, I asked? No one was really that inconvenienced or endangered. Suddenly instead of seeing stupid law breakers, I saw a line of human beings trying to enjoy a day out with one another, just like me. I realized that my vow of Lent to take my faith more seriously, more contemplatively meant taking off my narrowly focused lenses of judgment and replacing them with the wider vision of God's patient graciousness.

Choosing to be big about faith means choosing to live with and understand its consequences. It means humbly standing alone and making known the decisions of faith. It means not cheating when everyone else is, or not joining in on fun that you know is destructive to the reputation of someone else, or not accepting a contract which may be legal in the letter of the law while blatantly violating the spirit of the law. Refusing to be small about faith means not signing your name to poison pen documents and letters, writings that defame, overstate, and cruelly vilify all in the name of truth.

Choosing to be big about faith means granting forgiveness instead of striving to get even. It means being the first to walk away from meaningless conflict, especially when you know you have the strength to win. It means giving those you prove wrong dignified avenues of retreat instead of gloating over your victory. When you treat others as God's children, even when they don't return the favor, you are choosing to be big about faith.

When China finally allowed the outside world a glimpse into its life since the beginning of Communism, many were shocked to find what had happened to the Christian faith. Instead of shriveling up as the state had planned for it to do, it had increased dramatically and was robust beyond anything the missions to China had ever dreamed. When the state ordered all believers to adhere to the state run church, most of these Christians refused, and to this day carry on their faith in clandestine gatherings. To them it is worth risking trouble with their oppressive state in order to freely relate to the God who called them all brothers and sisters of Christ. The state is unable to comprehend what this faith gives these people that it cannot offer, and why they choose to make it such a big thing in their lives, even risking arrest because of it.

Jesus demonstrated what it meant by his actions in the temple. He was willing to take a relationship with God so seriously that he risked a huge public scene to make known how big this relationship was supposed to be.

Why not spend your Lenten season choosing to be big about your faith and your relationship to God!

Only God Owns the Weed Whacker

July 17, 2005

There is a wonderful gardening tool, rightfully called a weed whacker that many of us have used in the constant pursuit of the perfect lawn and the picture perfect flower garden. Most of the work involves getting rid of old weeds. A weed is defined as any living plant that is flourishing where a person doesn't want it to grow. Pity the poor plants that never seem to enjoy human favor such as dandelions and chickweed.

One day in 1971, a man named George Ballas was living in Houston, Texas and was striving to turn his lawn into the perfect lawn – a thing of exquisite beauty. What annoyed him most was that the grass grew in very hard to mow places, like around gnarled tree roots and between planter boxes. While pondering the problem, he came up with a homemade solution. He took an empty popcorn tin, punched some holes in it and then threaded in fishing lines. He somehow attached the contraption to his lawn edger and it quickly did the job. Later, Ballas and a machinist friend refined the devise and lo, the weed whacker was born.

I had experience using a weed whacker during our church workdays. I learned one important fact: this is not the device one gives to someone who knows nothing about plants and tells them to go to work. The outside of the box tells me it draws 5 amps of power at optimum performance, is very light weight and trims a 14" circle in a moment. It requires quickly spotting the difference between weeds and shrubbery.

Jesus said to let the weeds grow with the wheat; some weeds can be eaten or used as fuel to cook the meal. In our spiritual lives, we are to respect the plants that look like weeds. In fact, weeds may have an important place in what we harvest.

Before you use the weed whacker on the traits in your children and family that annoy you, look at them as something positive, something you can help them master and preserve. Before you use the weed whacker on yourself, be careful that you don't whack out a special plant that will grow and become a unique and blessed gift to your family and the world.

Take it easy with the weed whacker on your friends and colleagues. The plant you whack away may contain the seeds for a wonderful transformation that you are not equipped to envision or comprehend. Before you whack the plans and schemes that vex you in your life, think of how much they will enrich the harvest and make usable food for your soul.

We should let God alone own and operate the weed whacker. Our mission, our time and talent are to mind the growing of the wheat, and in trusting God for a bountiful harvest.

When the Sidewalk Ends

December 16, 2001

Sister Maureen Cahill was a nun who worked at a remote mission clinic in Northern Transvaal, South Africa. She used to tell a parable she called the parable of the pencil. It goes like this.
The inventor of the pencil addressed his finished product as follows:

> "I want you to remember four things:
> First your goodness or true worth is within you; secondly, you'll need to be sharpened as you go through life; thirdly, you'll be in someone else's hand, otherwise you'll make an awful mess; and finally, you'll be expected to leave a mark."

This gives us a way to keep our journey of faith on a meaningful track as our lives unfold before us and we find ourselves traveling beyond the sidewalk.

Let us remember that the meaning Jesus made clear is that God's love has bestowed a priceless value on each one of us. This is the point of the incarnation. God became human so that humans can claim the divinity that dwells in them. Human beings can choose to live manifesting the divine, or denying it. It's our choice.

We must remember that this value God invests in us resides

in every other human being, no matter how terrible they act or how much negativity they direct toward us.

I think it is very important to remember this as our country is engaged in a conflict with the Taliban and AI Qaeda. We will have to be wise about what sort of radicals we can allow to live among us and preserve a sane security. And we will have to do it with great caution. It is unsettling to know that those most fervently seeking the end of our way of life probably may not have taken that path if there had been caring individuals willing to do something about poverty, ignorance, and want. It may be too late to change these solidified intentions to "get us" and we will be left only with the hard choices of incarceration and execution. These experiences remind us of the great task we have of recognizing worth both inside and outside of the comfort of our own culture.

We need to claim the great worth God has put into all human life in the incarnation.

I have noticed that when the Olympics are announced on television, they highlight the winners exclusively. It's as though no one else exists save those who have won the gold, silver and bronze medals; and among those, of course the gold is always highlighted.

It is important in our life journey to remember that if God were to announce the Olympics you would hear a very different contest indeed. You would see scenes of non-medal winners who live through great struggle and loss; those who demonstrate the courage to go on despite the loss and despite the realization that the gold, silver and bronze are not attainable. You would see God hold up this kind of courage and faith and self-acceptance as the model for the spirit of sportsmanship. It is the spirit which aids us on our journey instead of hindering our progress.

Whenever you coach soccer, or baseball, or discuss sports with your kids next year, be mindful of what benefits God would have them get out of it. It may be a year in which many voices will tell you that you are not adequate for the job. You might be faced with a stalled career and a downturn in finances. Your children may hit rough spots and make you embarrassed to be their parents. You'll hear the negative voices of the demons -- yes, there really are demons! They can bring discouraging thoughts and sickness to your soul and keep up the constant dialogue about how you really aren't the person your dog thinks you are.

These are the voices of doubt which demean the great worth God has granted your soul. They will say to you, "you're not measuring up as a successful person. You're not a good parent like the parents whose kids are going to a real university. You're not the best salesman in your group, or the best office manager. So, go ahead, be depressed, be mad, be out of sorts and then go home and take it out on your rebellious daughter."

Nero was a terrible Emperor of Rome during the early Christian era. He was obsessed with his own power and believed he alone was the center of the civilized universe. His judgment was final when he decided a person's worth or lack of it. He was vain and ruthless and levied humiliation and torture on anyone he chose.

What he probably didn't realize was that in his very midst there were a group of people who simply didn't buy the idea that a mere mortal could determine their ultimate worth. Paul identified them when he finished his letter to the church at Philippi and said greetings were sent to them by the Christians who were in the court of Nero. Poor deluded Nero, thinking he could conquer the world when he had those in his court who shielded and respected their inner value that he thought he had won by force. Later they would prove that not even the threat of death could make them believe differently.

Keep in mind those dedicated Christians in the court of Nero and how they knew their worth and wouldn't let the power of Nero scare it out of them. Remember them when your inner Nero demon wants to tell you how small you are, how worthless you have become, or how useless your gifts are to anyone.

The pencil must expect to be sharpened. This means that our journeys of faith are going to be full of times when we will have to suffer through hard lessons and sharpening to make us aware of what is truly important. Expect to suffer losses. Awareness of the reality of loss makes us value those who are near us. It makes us more awake to the moment and less prone to living in a kind of dream world full of mythical expectations of earthly immortality and invulnerability.

When Elizabeth and Zechariah raised their son John, it's pretty clear that they raised a very intense young man who took the religious fervor to places Zechariah was not comfortable to go. Wearing camel skins, living in caves, eating locusts and honey and becoming a legendary figure loved by the people and feared by the authorities, John the Baptist was probably his parents' greatest worry. I can hear them in their old age saying to him, "John, John, when are you going to settle down, get a family, get a REAL job. This isn't the life we wanted for you."

I'm sure the life they wanted for him probably wasn't the journey of faith he chose. And accepting this fact was part of the pencil sharpening the parents had to do in their own lives to accept their son's unusual vocation.

The inventor tells the pencil that it needs to expect to be in someone else's hand or it will not function. God calls us into faith communities because God knows that we are at our best in groups. In this sense our journey of faith always sees us in the hands of others. If we are to really find the wisdom life affords us and go where God would have us go, we need the gathered wisdom and reflected knowledge of others.

It's interesting how learning language is something we do best as children. We are at our most teachable when we are in a pliable childish state. When Jesus said that the greatest in the Kingdom of Heaven is the one who humbles himself and become like a child, he refers to being open to the teaching of God as a child is open to learning from others. If we do not let the hands of others guide us and take counsel of only our own limited wisdom we will never gain our full spiritual potential.

Finally, the pencil's inventor tells it that it needs to make a mark. A pencil is built for writing, drawing and creating. Our lives have been created for serving God, manifesting God's love to the world around us once we have caught the vision of God's love living in us. Making our mark means expressing this love of God. Each of us has our own sheet of the paper of life to make our mark upon.

I end this with the wisdom of an anonymous English source as words to ponder when the sidewalk ends on your faith journey this year.

I asked God for strength that I might achieve;
   I was made weak that I might learn humbly to obey.

I asked for help that I might do greater things;
   I was given infirmity that I might do better things.

I asked for riches that I might be happy;
   I was given poverty that I might be wise.

I asked for all things that I might enjoy life;

82 The Soul's Journey

I was given life that I might enjoy all things.

I was given nothing that I asked for;
But everything that I had hoped for.

Despite myself, my prayers were answered;
I am among all men most richly blessed.

The Third Eye

October 1, 2001

Prayer is meant to focus us on what is near to us so that we do not miss the details of our lives; the small blessings, the instances of the presence of God in people and events which are common, but nonetheless holy. Prayer and meditation are also meant to focus us on the distant, the greater love and harmony of God which stretches beyond the boundaries of the universe. In this way we focus beyond the perimeter of our own lives and experience, placing ourselves in the larger context of God's love and grace without feeling lost or diminished.

When James exhorted Christians to stop signing their promises with an oath involving God, he probably wanted Christians to give up the practice of treating God as the Lord of magic tricks. God is not turned on or off by incantations, or spoken formulas which invoke his power to do one's bidding. Yet in our childish ways, we often start our prayers in this way.

Marvin Barret, a Harvard trained writer, tells us how he began his prayer life with disastrous results. In his article in *Parabola* entitled, *"Praying in the World,"* Barret writes this:

"I began my prayers at age three... Then at age eight, petitions and intercessions converged and prayer as I knew it was wiped out by an instant, unambiguous, and soul-destroying answer. The Deity had heard and granted a thoughtless request with a terrifying promptness."

Barret says this because he prayed that his three-year-old brother, Edwin would die. He was not only unbearably jealous of his little brother, but also coveted all the toys he would inherit after his demise. A short hour after uttering this selfish prayer, his brother was struck and killed by a car while in Barret's care.

The awful reality of what had happened horrified young Marvin.

"For a day or two my prayers continued: that he would be brought back, that what I had seen at the top of the hill was an evil dream, that he was there at the other end of our attic room asleep in his trundle bed, that God would understand I hadn't meant it."

At the funeral, he was made to gaze upon his little brother's body. He writes,

"I was led up to the satin-lined coffin and forced, resisting looking in. He was peaceful and beautiful and still, terrifyingly still. His auburn curls were more ordered than they ever had been in life: his lips fashioned into a seraphic smile, his cheeks flushed with an earthly, waxy glow. I looked and was appalled. I screwed my eyes closed and vowed never to pray again."

It wasn't until 14 years later, after Marvin had earned a scholarship to Harvard and won multiple academic honors that prayer came back into his life. It happened when he was in the Navy during the Second World War, and discovered that Aldous Huxley, one of the great literary favorites of his agnostic adolescence (as he puts it), had become the promoter of "wall to wall, center-to-center meaning, his preferred access to this dazzling revelation, being prayer."

Amazed at this shift from Huxley's role as "the apostle of clever meaninglessness," Barret began to read the writings of the man who had inspired Huxley to return to a life of prayer and faith. In this journey, Marvin Barret again found the presence of God, the grace of Christ, and the power of prayer and meditation to shape his life and restore it.

In doing so he found that prayer has essentially two parts. The first part is meditation and the second is spoken, or petition, the seeking of God's grace and love for people, events, one's own understanding.

In meditation he learned the truth of putting God first. Meditation is the practice of emptying the conscious mind of all things, and allowing God to move in at will. Meditation is not the attempt to be a good person, to right certain wrongs with oneself, or anyone else. It is the act of a human seeking communion with the presence of God.

Prayer begins with meditation, an emptying of the self; and a quiet opening of the soul to the radiant presence of God's love and grace. It then moves to words, spoken in the honesty which is afforded the soul that is centered in the gracious assurance of God's love and forgiveness.

The reason the most effective, life-shaping praying begins with meditation, is that this act opens us up to a new insight which is not tangled up with the promptings of our own ego.

Many have described this new insight as a kind of vision let into the soul by a spiritual eye, which opens when we exercise its muscles in quiet, God-centered meditation. This is meditation which practices a strict focus on God. It works on detachment from the ego and its needs that propel us with a multitude of desires, most of which are unnecessary for spiritual strength and insight.

When we do finally come to our prayers of petition, they are prayers which seek to do the work God gives us. They are petitions to fulfill God's will through our actions, our thoughts, and our behavior. Hugh Gilbert, abbot of Pluscarden Abby of Scotland, put it well during an interview when he said, "Through praise, it is an acknowledgment of what God has done and is doing, and through intercession, it is striving to complete that work in historical circumstances and in the here and now."

Prayer begins with the opening of the eye of the soul to the presence of God, unobstructed by the desires of the ego. It surveys the world through the lenses of divine grace and compassion. And it then shapes our will to do that which can bring God's love into human experience. We find that prayer from hearts informed by the open eye of the soul cannot pray for distracting things like good outcomes to car deals, or a better parking place.

Former New York Yankee player, Yogi Berra once experienced this reality when during a ball game, which was tied with two outs in the bottom of the 9th inning, a batter from the opposing team stepped up to the plate where Berra was catching. He looked around and made the sign of the cross on home plate with the bat. Berra was a good Catholic too, but as he wiped off the plate with his glove, he said to the pious batter, "Why don't we let God just watch this game?"

The prayer of the contemplating heart seeks the wisdom to

act, not the excuse to let God act for it. It prays this prayer
recorded by Rev. James Hewitt:

We cannot merely pray to you, O God, to end war;
For we know that you have made the world in a way
That man must find his own path to peace
Within himself and with his neighbor.
We cannot merely pray to you, O God, to end starvation;
For you have given us the resources
With which to feed the entire world
If we would only use them wisely.
We cannot merely pray to you, O God,
To root out prejudice,
For You have already given us eyes
With which to see the good in all people
If we would only use them rightly.
We cannot merely pray to You, O God, to end despair,
For You have already given us the power
To clear away slums and give hope
If we would only use our power justly.
We cannot merely pray to You, O God, to end disease,
For you have already given us great minds with which
To search out cures and healing,
If we would only use them constructively,
Therefore, we pray to You instead, O God,
For Strength, determination, and willpower,
To do, instead of just to pray,
To become, instead of merely to wish.

Amen

Walking the Walk of Christ

February 11, 2001
125th Anniversary Sunday

Ephesians 5:1-5,15-20

In the 5th chapter of Paul's letter to the churches of Asia Minor called Ephesians, he tries to speak from his heart about how the followers of Christ should express the love of Christ to each other and to the world. He echoed this in Chapter 4 where he wrote,

> "I, therefore, a prisoner of the Lord, beg you to lead a life worthy of the calling to which you have been called, with all lowliness and meekness, with patience, forbearing one another in love, eager to maintain the unity of the Spirit in the bond of peace."

He begins Chapter 5 trying to give the people some guidance on how to mold their characters to the new identity in Christ. So he says, "Therefore be imitators of God, as beloved children. And walk in love, as Christ loved us and gave himself up for us, a fragrant offering and sacrifice to God."

The picture painted in this first verse is that of people trying to imitate the walk of Christ. The Greek word "*peripateo*" means "walk about ... or tread all around." So, the sentence means to walk like Jesus did.

Verse 15 picks up this walking illustration when it says, "Look carefully then how you live and walk (*peripateo*), and don't walk as unwise people do, but walk like wise people, making the most of the time you have on earth."

A friend of mine, Rev. Shel White, told me that when he was a very young boy, he developed a detached retina. In those days the answer to a treatment for this problem involved days of laying in a hospital absolutely still, hoping that the doctor's work on the detached retina would heal. So he lay there in a hospital bed, a small boy totally blinded by the bandages that had been wrapped over both of his eyes during the healing process.

During this hard time, Shel remembered being unable to see people, but being able to tell who they were and judge who was coming to see him by the sound of their walking. He could tell who was walking by his door by the cadence, and the weight of their footsteps, and each person's distinct walk.

One nurse used to enter his room like a freight train. He could hear her heavy, clomping feet far up the hallway as she neared his room. Then she would burst in banging the door, moving heavily to his bed, shaking the floor, and greeting him in a loud, somewhat raspy voice, "Hi Shel."

So out of the daily experience of this particular nurse's great strength, communicated by sound, Shel formed a picture of her in his head. Each day he could hear her coming clear down the hallway, banging into his room and rasping, "Hi Shel." And each time his picture of a large, robust woman became more defined in his imagination.

When the bandages were removed and Shel could see people for the first time, he heard her coming down the hall. He eagerly awaited the first sight he would have of her large form, happily thudding into his room like a locomotive through a small snowdrift. Soon she was there, bustling through the banging door. His mouth fell open when he saw the smallest, most petite, and girlish of all the nurses, with a diminutive little mouth that uttered a huge, raspy "Hi Shel."

A walk can say more about what we are than our looks.

Paul wanted people to understand that they were redeemed people, loved for the separate personalities they were. But he also wanted them to know that it is possible for a person who has met the wonderful love of God in Jesus Christ, to assimilate the love of Christ into one's personality, like one would consciously try to assimilate the walk of another person. Over time, this assimilation is not put on, but becomes an actual part of the personality of the person.

So Paul is saying to us, add to your unique personality the walk of Christ. Include the walk of love of yourself, of your neighbor, of nature, the grace of Christ, and the forgiveness of Christ. Just as you would copy a person's walk, copy these traits of Christ, and they will in time, become your traits, and their blessings will be your blessings.

When I was in the 3rd grade, I had a best friend named Jimmy Armstrong. Jimmy was fun to be around because he was active and we shared the same interests. He was athletic, outgoing, and confident. He was also very kindhearted and mellow and was a popular fellow, liked by both girls and boys. Whenever a captain for a kick ball team was needed, Jimmy was chosen. And he was never smug about his ability; he was just good at most sports, and enjoyed them. He was both a good winner and a good loser.

Jimmy had one problem. He had a knee injury which appeared to be permanent. It partially restricted the motion in his right leg, so he walked and ran with a limp. The handicap definitely slowed him down, but he was still a great little athlete. Like so many in my third grade class, I admired Jimmy, and felt really lucky that we were best friends and spent so much time after school together.

I admired Jimmy so much, that I even admired his limp. I thought it was really cool; it made him look like a battle-hardened veteran, a man of the world. Secretly, I wished for Jimmy's limp. Once Jimmy and a neighbor boy climbed onto the roof of Jimmy's house, and the neighbor challenged Jimmy to jump off. I could see that Jimmy wasn't eager to meet this challenge, and I thought that the injured leg was probably the main reason he didn't want to participate in this game of chicken.

It bothered me that the neighbor kid was unaware or insensitive to Jimmy's reluctance to jump, and perhaps not be so quick in making one leg work when hitting the ground. So to help my friend I quickly climbed onto the roof, told the little neighbor kid to watch and follow if he dared, and popped off the roof.

On the way down I remembered how much I hated heights. When I landed, hit the ground and rolled, I discovered my loathing was with great merit. I put on a brave face, but only I knew my right knee was screaming for mercy. It was only after the neighbor boy went home, declining to follow my flight; I let Jimmy know that I now walked with a limp too.

I was extremely proud of my limp. For a week we limped together, until gradually mine faded, and I was left only with a memory of our shared glory, and my everlasting admiration of this best friend. But for a glorious week I walked like Jimmy, and felt what it was like to be confident like him.

I was speechless the day Jimmy told me he was going to move. In fact I repressed the fact until the day I arrived at his house to find it almost empty, and Jimmy saying good-bye, with his mother standing behind him. His mother said something very strange to me. She said she was truly grateful that I had been Jimmy's friend because it had meant so much to Jimmy, and to her. Jimmy, she said, admired the things I did and how I did them.

I barely heard her, because I was fighting to keep the lump in my chest from dissolving into my throat and up into my tear ducts. At the time, I couldn't understand what she had meant. In my eyes, Jimmy Armstrong was the perfect person, replete with a cool limp I would put up with pain to imitate, and a personality I would always in some way emulate in my own actions.

Years later as an adult, I understood what she had meant. To her, Jimmy was her wounded child. He was the boy she worried over because she was concerned that his handicap would make him feel diminished. My adulation of Jimmy had been a great relief to her. Apparently Jimmy had admired my own athletic ability with two whole legs, and was given confidence by my adulation of his restricted ability. Jimmy's mom was letting me know that while I was putting on Jimmy's walk, he was putting on mine, and we were both the better for it.

So let us do as Paul said: let us put on Christ, as I had put on Jimmy's walk, and as he had put on mine. This experience teaches us that we can share the wholeness of our own personal redemptions with others, so that their inner pain and doubts and personal losses can be turned into victories.

Let us ask ourselves if we are walking in love as Christ walked, so that our neighbors, our children and grandchildren, younger associates, friends and business contacts feel redemption and wholeness in our presence. It doesn't matter if you live with a limp -- if you live by the gracious love of Christ. Remember how much a small third grade boy admired his friend's limp, and boldly share with thanksgiving your limping life with the world. The little Jimmies of the world who are affected by us will want to put on our walk, because we walk in Christ.

Shelving the Survivalist Self

February 18, 2001

Each day we arise with the possibility of living in our spiritual being or our other being, the self-centered, survivalist being. Though we might choose to live spiritually, we are very soon challenged to behave otherwise. I discovered this on Thursday mornings when I would travel to my sermon group. I was always traveling in heavy commute traffic, although it is even heavier going in the opposite direction.

By the time I got to the interstate highway my resolve to live the redeemed, spiritual life, was beginning to be tested by that now familiar state of mind called road rage.

I noticed there was a commuter lane on the far left lane of the highway and each Thursday I would drive in the lane next to it, often creeping along as drivers with more than one passenger sped past me. I resisted the urge to pull into the lane and take my chances. Because, I reasoned, I am a law-abiding person; I don't deserve that lane unless I have a passenger. And just as I think this, whoosh, a car with one lone individual in it would streak past me. I always imagine the driver smirking, his or her head bobbing to mindless music on a too loud radio.

I feel the rage rise in me. I fantasize - the police car appearing out of nowhere and pursuing the now frightened violator, handing him that fat fine advertised on the sign sticking up out of the highway divider. Before long, I was consumed with the action going on in the commuter lane. I was deaf to the wonderful music I was playing on the CD; I was blind to the beauty of nature painted in the clouds and shafts of sunlight edging them with fire. All of my attention was riveted to watching the car that has just sped past in the commuter lane, counting heads, wondering if there WAS another head behind that headrest. I found myself frequently glancing in the rear view side mirror, trying to see if the next car in the commuter lane contained a single occupant. I grew suspicious: I suspected dummies, fake child seats, or coats folded to look like dozing heads. I became the watchman of the commuter lane, the grim judge of all who passed, seething with negative hopes for all who do not pass my vigilant scrutiny.

It was absolutely exhausting. I would arrive at the sermon group edged with combativeness and negativity. All of that work judging offenders really did affect the way I thought, acted, created, and responded. It was poison for my relationships, my thinking, and my soul.

Jesus taught, If you learn to love the people who annoy you, and even those who outright oppose you, everything will be viewed differently. When you stop living in constant judgment, feeling you're the commuter lane judge of the world, passing judgment on all those folk who are trapped in their baser selves, you'll find yourself finally at peace. When you do this, Jesus says your reward will be magnificent and you'll have that sensation which comes when you really understand that you are not just a meaningless blob of protoplasm. You're a child of the Most High, the God whose name is too holy to be contained in mere earthly expression.

Blessings and Curses

May 12, 2002

The members of my family, who bear the name Nebo, all love to talk. This is especially true of the men of my family: my brother, their sons, at least most of them, my late half brother, and as far as I can tell, my late father. There is a blessing in this talent for being talkers. We talkers are capable of keeping the party going, we can entertain with our streams of friendly words and long stories. We are blessed with the ability to converse with most fellow beings who speak our language, and some who don't. When a group needs a spokesperson, someone with the ability to speak on their feet and respond to questions of the moment, we talkers are called upon to use the blessed talent we have for filling the room with words, no matter how tense the situation.

But there is another side to this picture. The blessing is balanced with a curse. At its core, this curse becomes the inability to listen because we are so driven to talk. When a threatening situation cries out for some calm, focused receptivity, we talkers are instead trapped in a frantic flood of words, spilling over the dam of restraint, with the hope of flushing down river whatever it is that is bothering us. We are the people who can't keep a sermon to 20 minutes and who ignore the need to stop talking and just say goodbye.

My wife was my reserved opposite. She was spare on words and throughout our marriage was a balance to my loquacious nature. There were times when she loved my gift of gab. But there were times when I could tell that she considered it a cross she would bear because she loved me. On the other hand, I encouraged her to tell me what she thought and felt, and I became the balance to her quieter nature. Once when I complained that she was giving me great distress in her criticism of my verbosity, she said wisely, "Yes, I am your love and your critic. I am your wife to extract from you your better nature." I answered hotly at the time, "And so I'll be your husband and do the same for you, right?" She just smiled and said, "I'm telling you in words what I think, like you tell me you need me to do, so I guess that's true."

My wife, whom I loved so much, spent 30 years lovingly helping me to extract from my nature my blessings and to redeem the curses.

When we celebrate baptism, we acknowledge one of life's most formative forces; the relationship we have or have had with our mothers. For some, those relationships are filled with stories of the extracting of blessings and for others they are painfully overfilled with the memories of trying to redeem curses. Let us look at the intimate relationship God wants to have with us; a relationship as close as we have had or wished we had had with our mothers. And as we look at that relationship we will see how God desires that we allow the love, and his compassion to guide us to extract from our natures the blessings, and redeem the curses.

The story of Jacob and Joseph is a retelling that has many layers of meaning. One of its layers is that it demonstrates how a family struggles to understand itself in light of the purposes of God. It is a study of the redemption of the family's curses and the extraction of its blessings.

Jacob was born to a father and mother who loved all their children. Unfortunately, this love was influenced by the curse of the propensity to choose favorites.   Isaac favored the athleticism of Esau and Rebekah favored the cleverness of her son, Jacob. To her son, Rebekah gave the blessing of the gift of discerning how the community functioned and what one could do to control the process. At its best it was a means to diplomacy. At its worst it was the curse of manipulation and covert rule. It was the latter that got Jacob into trouble after his mother contrived the receiving of his father's blessing, which now-blind Isaac had meant to give to Esau. Certainly, some of this had to do with the customs of the times, but I suspect part of the problem stemmed from the fact that father and mother never challenged each other so that they could lovingly extract from their marriage their blessings and redeem their curses.

This failure to work with the grace of God to confront the blessings and curses of their personalities and family life ended with Jacob fleeing his brother's anger and taking refuge with his Uncle Leban.

Later in the story, we find Jacob a widower with 12 sons. His sons carry within them variations of the same blessings and curses. The great blessing of his son Joseph, the blessing of discerning dreams, becomes a curse when he insensitively reveals the content of one of his dreams to his jealous brothers -- the dream that he would become ruler and they would be his subjects. Joseph's brothers, having not yet extracted the blessings from their lives, took the kind of action Esau would have taken. They deposited little Joseph down a deep well and eventually sold him to a passing band of desert merchants.

The brothers, equally masters of deception, provided a ruse complete with Joseph's distinctive cloak dipped in animal blood to convince their father that lions had devoured Joseph. Ironic, isn't it? The family history, begun when Jacob deceived his own father, tragically continued as his sons desperately sought to deceive him. The Bible presents us with a family, which in some ways is much like our own families, i.e. wonderful mixtures of love and pain, seeking God's help in extracting the blessings and redeeming the curses.

Joseph discovered that the dream that portrayed him as ruler and his brothers as his subjects meant that he would bring the family the means to live through a dangerous famine. The dream had nothing to do with God declaring him superior over his brothers. All of this became clear at the end of the story, when all of the brothers, then grown men, finally confronted the curses they had visited upon each other. Joseph confessed his deception, and his love for his brothers. His brothers expressed their regret and the true complex story of all that had happened in their journey through the years was revealed.

It is a story of a family discovering in their very humanness the blessing of grace and forgiveness, compassion and mercy. It is a story of the redemption of the curse of deception and manipulation by the power of love and relationship, and the desire to follow God's will.

When Nicodemus said to Jesus that he wanted to know what the secret was to obtaining eternal life, Jesus told him simply that he had to be born again. He had to start over and see himself as totally stripped of any accomplishments. He had to see himself as starting his life again with the basic premise that the gifts of breath and sight, respiration, and strength contained in his DNA were the loving possession of God. He was not an accident. He was Nicodemus, child of God, who was given the blessed gift of life.

Jesus saw in Nicodemus the core-individual. He didn't see the man who was a powerful scholar, and a respected officer of the temple. Jesus recognized something that transcended all of the honors and titles Nicodemas had won from his culture. He saw the value of the essence of this man, and wanted him to understand that God loved his center being, that which was truly blessed about him and would be so forever. This blessedness was expressed in both Nicodemus's success, but it was equally expressed in his failures. The only way he could appreciate this experience was to begin with no assumptions of his worth and realize that God loved him for who he was inside, not for the shell of attributes celebrated in his titles, his accomplishments, and his victories.

Baptism is the fundamental ritual acknowledging the truth that Jesus presented to Nicodemus. God sees us for what we are and God loves us for that core value we have in the eyes of God. God blesses us with talents that have two sides, both positive and negative. By acknowledging our positive side we gain strength and confidence. By acknowledging our negative side, we gain the power of humility. Confidence and humility are the two eyes of the soul. Without both of them we cannot see reality in three dimensions. Without both of them we will always see the world in a distorted way. Again, we confront our blessings and curses.

We are all born again Christians if we embrace the message of Christ and accept the truth of what he said to us about our core natures.   In that blessed truth, Jesus gives us the confidence to bring to him our lives and with the aid of the grace of God, extract from them our blessings and redeem our curses. In that way, we progress from a newborn babe in Christ to spiritual adulthood.

A young man once proposed to his girlfriend as they sat looking over a beautiful lake on a moon lit night. "Darling, I want you to know that I love you more than anything else in the world. I want you to marry me. I'm not wealthy. I don't have a yacht or a Rolls-Royce like Johnny Green, but I do love you with all my heart."

She thought for a minute and then replied, "I love you with all my heart too, but tell me more about Johnny Green."

It is easy to see the young woman was interested in what Johnny Green possessed, not who he was. Perhaps she has a talent for acquiring wealth, which is her blessing. At the same time she will have to see that if not corralled, this blessing could become the curse of materialism and undermine the roots of her spiritual well being

Rebekah had the great ability to understand her husband and sons and to act so that obstacles could be removed. But like the young woman who was curious about Johnny Green's wealth, Rebekah found her blessing could be a curse if it was not executed in the light of God's love and meaning for her life. Isaac loved his sons, which was his blessing, but his love was cursed with favoritism; his failure to face the inconsistency in his love, and not to anticipate the results of his actions, created tragedy for his sons.

We are born again when we accept the reality of Christ, his life, death and resurrection. And we are meant to develop as the beloved babes of God's love to mature adults. We do this by allowing the living spirit of God to enlighten us so that we wisely examine our lives truthfully, extracting from them our blessings and truthfully naming and redeeming our curses.

Each of our blessings is watchful for the curse it might need to redeem.

Blessing of talkativeness looks to redeem the curse of not listening.
Blessing of serenity, watches for the curse of inaction.
Blessing of positive activeness watches for the curse of destructive
        aggression.
Blessing of patience watches for the curse of victimization.
Blessing of instructing one's child watches for the curse of immaturity.
Blessing of good fortune watches for the curse of debilitating pride.

So let us celebrate what God has done for us and extract from our lives the blessings of ourselves, and truthfully enjoy the redemption of our curses.

This was taken in San Fernando, the last year with our foster parents. Jack was in the 7th grade and I was in the 6th grade.

Double Vision on the Fourth of July

July 4, 1999

In the 13th chapter of Luke a story is told of Jesus healing a woman who was bent over and in great discomfort, possibly from arthritis, or osteoporosis. The story does not say whether the woman approached Jesus to do anything for her, but when Jesus caught sight of her, painfully bent over and partially immobile, he was touched in his heart. He immediately called to her, placed his hands on her, and healed her.

The ruler of the synagogue, a man of power and influence, probably resentful because he did not have the power to do as Jesus did, criticized Jesus for working on the Sabbath, the holy day of rest.

After declaring the Sabbath an appropriate day to lift the terrible burdens of people, he tells the parable of the mustard seed. Jesus declares that faith in God is supposed to be like a mustard seed which people plant in their lives. Its purpose is to grow, and grow, until it becomes a beautiful tree full of life, providing soothing shade for the traveler, and a habitat for nature's creatures.

In another correlation, faith is like the leaven in bread dough. It may be small, but its purpose is to affect the entire piece of dough so that it rises to its full potential and becomes a fragrant, nourishing loaf of bread. The purpose of the bread is to feed the world with spiritual goodness; it is to fill us with respect for the sacristy of life, appreciation of human relationships, beauty, mercy, justice, and creativity.

As I write this, it is Sunday, the fourth of July. It is a day in which I will partake in two separate acts of devotion. In one I will break a loaf of bread, pour the fruit of the vine in ceremonial cups and declare that the Spiritual presence of Christ is in us as we partake in the very nature of God. The act of Communion will bring forth that vision of God in us, by seeking to purify our motives, our actions, and our very selves. We will share bread and the fruit of the vine knowing that life is sacred, and that God desires humans to live in loving peace with each other.

The other act of devotion is less focused, but nonetheless important. It is a time to set off fireworks, listen to patriotic speeches and rousing music celebrating the vision of an independent America based on democracy and individual freedom.

The one act is sacred. The other act is secular. Citing the doctrine of separation of church and state, many believe they should be kept separate. The doctrine was formulated in the minds of men and women who told the monarch of England that his loyal subjects were henceforth going to be loyal to the power of majority rule. It was the logical outcome of the idea that God did not give power to one individual, but rather that he gave equal worth to all. Hence power was more rightly derived from the popular will. It is not difficult to understand why these same minds concluded that no single religious body should hold state power. They had experienced religious persecution as Huguenots in France, as non-conformist Puritans in England, as Catholics in Switzerland. They did not wish to continue these religious upheavals in their fledgling state. They did not want to live under the constant threat of being tyrannized by someone who claimed his domination was righteous because he was God's chosen instrument of rule.

It was not the intent of those early founders of the American vision to establish a commitment to ignorance about religious life. Nor was it their intent to preclude people of religious conviction from making public policy from the dictates of their faith-informed consciences. What is required of them is that they obtain a majority vote to do it, and that their actions not infringe on the civil or religious rights of others.

Those early founders of the great experiment called Democracy, struggled to form a new vision from the raw materials of their hard experiences in the old world and frighteningly new experiences in the new continent. We know it was not a complete vision. It did not include people of color, and it left women out of the vision as well. It took a civil war, and years of racial strife to bring about the enfranchisement of people of color. It took the women's marches of this century and the movement of the last 40 years to bring us to an awareness of what equality in gender is all about. And we are still learning about the implications of this experiment called Democracy.

Today, let us use both the vision of our faith, and the vision of our national life to create one vision of what we might become in the future as a people. Let us look to the road ahead through two eyes - one using our secular sight and the other our faith sight. Together they give us the depth perception we need. It is only with this vision that we can see our mustard seed grow to be a blessing to the world, and our leaven become the dough of life. The bread that comes forth can feed more than our own needs.

I would like to share with you some of my thoughts on the double vision of the future of our faith, and the future of our nation.

I envision a time when our public schools do not shy away from religious discussion, but rather relish it. Instead of saying that Puritans came to this country for a better life, I dream of a time when students are informed as to what theological thought and impulses drove people from England to Holland and finally to our shores where they sought to set up a theocracy, not a democracy. I dream of a curriculum that helps students understand why Moslem Americans desire to make the Hajj so fervently. I dream of classrooms with enough curiosity and appreciation of religious difference that teachers will not fear to have a student who has made a Hajj tell others why he went and what it meant to him. I envision Christian and Mormon students free to discuss why they have chosen to spend a summer on a church mission, and Jewish students invited by their Moslem and Christian counterparts to say why seeing Jerusalem is so meaningful to them.

I envision a time when Christians and Jews, Moslems and Hindus and Buddhists take seriously the spirit shown by the Dalai Lama, when he described the good heart of faith; the heart which does not take offense upon meeting another faith, but concentrates in finding instruction and growth. This means that Christians would study Islam beyond its obvious disagreement over the place of women. And Islam would study Christianity without being detoured by the obvious Christian love of materialism. Each faith would instead try to understand the best intentions of the other, and then in appreciative dialogue, thankful for lessons each teaches the other, address differences with patience and good will. In time I believe that Islam will have to address its disparity with women; just as we Christians will have to face our addiction to materialism.

I envision a time when our nation finally addresses the notion that the earth is the Lords' and the fullness thereof. By this I mean that our nation will begin to see the earth and its resources as an organism with a sacred life it must preserve, not endlessly exploit without any thought of tomorrow. We cannot be serious about saving the whales while we wantonly destroy lesser life with out-of-control growth and development. We cannot be serious about saving the rain forest when we have not even made a great effort to reforest our suburban environment, a task still within our reach.

As a Christian, I envision a time when people in the corporate world hold regular, serious discussions about how the economic practices of our huge, global market sometimes crushes the fortunes of people in third-world countries and I dream of a time when these leaders strive to work in harmony with their governments to mend the practices and ameliorate their affects, because they see justice and compassion as good business.

I envision a time when all children of our country are taught at least one foreign language, Spanish, to make a common connection with the population of our side of the world. This would take place because children would want to engage in it, not because it was mandated by well-intentioned, but erroneous public policy.

I dream of a time when our seminaries require that students be fully educated in the key precepts of the world's five major religions in order to earn the degree of master or doctor of divinity. This would be accomplished by years of interaction with men and women who represent those diverse faith communities of Judaism, Buddhism, Islam, and Hinduism.

I envision a time when men and women cease to argue about their gender differences and accept each other for the diverse gifts they bring to the great challenges in the century to come. It would also be a time when sexual orientation could be accepted for the genetic development it usually is, its purpose in society identified and understood. This would allow us a society where sexual orientation would neither be discriminated against, nor irately and defensively flaunted.

I envision a time when the value of child rearing, and family life is respected and cherished. The role of family life in our society bears the sacred duty of instilling in our young the importance of love, loyalty and responsibility, and the meaning of God in our lives. This would mean that teachers would again be respected and honored, and their efforts well rewarded by a grateful public.

Finally, I envision a time when the noble ideal is returned to our sense of work. Doctors would be encouraged to see their work as sacred. Lawyers would become aware of the great, sacred trust that is delegated to them as they help us understand our place and standing before the law. Those who work in the home would be respected as vital parts in the life of our society; they would receive realistic appreciation and compensation for the tasks they do to serve us all, not just their own families.

Proverbs 29: 18, written over 2500 years ago says, "Where there is no vision, the people perish." I encourage you to use your double vision of faith and secular wisdom to form your visions of this country and your life in it.

In her book, **Samples of American Songs,** Maymie R. Krythe, wrote about Dr. Katherine Lee Bates, a vibrant and intelligent professor of English at Wellesley College. During the 1880s, Dr. Bates traveled from her native New England to make a grueling trip to the top of 14,000 foot Pikes Peak, a real eye opener for a native of the flatter Eastern part of the country. Out of this experience and her own religious convictions she wrote a poem which was later set to music and became the much loved song, *"America the Beautiful."*

Maymie Kryth wrote,

> "It was in the West that she got her first views of really wide-open spaces. When the poet realized all this abundance and vastness, she was inspired to pray that God would 'shed his grace' on this country, and that its people would live under laws, realizing that liberty is not license. Finally, she thinks of the problems of her own time; for example, the contrast of the magnificent Court of Honor, center of the Chicago World's fair, and the hovels in many city slums. Again, she prays that true brotherhood will bring about a better future for all America's citizens."

Look to the inspiring, hopeful words of *"America the Beautiful"* as a reminder to use our Christian faith as the mustard seed, and the leaven in the bread of life, and let our double vision guide our actions.

The Small Dot on the Bigger Paper

June 9, 2002

A Sunday school teacher once used this illustration:
She held up two pieces of white paper, one large, one small.
Each piece had the same sized black dot in the center. As the
students studied the two papers, they all agreed it was easier
to see the black dot on the smaller piece of paper.

I think of this illustration as a way of reminding us that the
Christian faith is about seeing the sights of our journey of this
life in the context of God's larger picture. We are wise to
notice the spots that appear on this picture, whether they are
the sinful acts of another person, or the extraordinarily saintly
acts of someone else. But it is wiser to remember that this
larger picture always has room to grow with more dots, and
that it is the promise of God that in the end these dots will
add up to something wonderful and meaningful. We forget
this when we get too attached to one set of dots or another.

When Jesus looked at humankind he always saw the larger
picture, the bigger sheet of paper. This was confusing to
people who were working so hard to be righteous and correct
in the eyes of God. Thousands of years of habit, custom,
contemplation and writing had gone into identifying the spots
that could tarnish the spiritual character of a human soul.
When Jesus appeared, he took time to see the larger sheet of
paper upon which the experience of grace could be written,
so that the old dots became a new set of habits and actions,

thoughts and beliefs. Without any great discussion of his spots, Jesus called Matthew, a hated tax collector to join his band of disciples. In the evening he broke bread with anyone, including those who were known for their impious habits.

When people around Jesus complained of this, he said simply that he had come to save the lost and sinful, not the righteous and secure. Of course he knew there was not a single human who did not have faults and a need to come to terms with the darker sides of themselves. They needed to be aware of the meaning of the love and grace of God, and to express it with humility and compassion to others.

When Jesus was discussing this spiritual truth, an officer of the synagogue came to him begging him to hurry to his daughter's bedside and heal her before the illness took her life. On the way to the officer's home, Jesus was stopped by a woman who was desperate to be healed of her continual hemorrhaging. She only touched the hem of his garment, but Jesus could feel the desperation of the touch. He was wise to the true needs of the moment, and knowing that an interruption in his plans could itself become his plans, he responded to her request.

Even the call for his attention to an important matter did not keep him from living in the bigger spiritual picture of God's grace. The picture said that the desperation of a woman in the crowd was worthy of interrupting his important task; it was worthy of a compassionate ear and a healing touch.

Like many others, I am a task driven person. When I feel a task is important I tend to make everything else secondary and drive for its completion. It is an old habit of concentrating on the black dots. In many ways, it is a good thing. It helps me accomplish much and many have been aided by it. Also, like many of you, I can be driven from the bigger sheet of paper by staring at the dots. Sometimes it is hard to remember that Jesus taught us to always remember this bigger sheet of paper. God has written the story of our individual lives on a sheet of paper that is big enough to encompass all the dots of everyone else's lives.

This means attending to the gift of time, thought and attention that people bring to us. For many years of my life I had never really thought about this until one fateful afternoon when I was attending seminary. At the time I lived off campus in an apartment complex in San Rafael and commuted to my part time jobs as a seminary assistant in a church in San Francisco, and a grouter in a decorative candleholder shop in San Rafael. So, when my car had a problem I was very motivated to make things right.

One day, as was my custom, I was under the car banging away at something and I was so intent upon what I was doing, that I didn't notice the feet of a little boy appear near my head. As I continued to work under the car, I heard a charming, childish voice talking to me. I assumed that he was really fascinated by all the banging that was going on, and curious about what I was doing. My first thought was to tell him that I was really busy trying to patch a hot exhaust pipe, without losing my fingerprints, so I couldn't talk much.

I began to realize this little tike wasn't at all interested in what I was doing. He wanted to tell me a story. In fact, he had launched into it and was blabbing away without any sign of stopping. I replied, in a strained happy voice, "How nice! Now run along while Mr. Mechanic tries to fix the hole in the sizzling pipe."

But he wouldn't stop talking. Then a sentence came like lightning through the cloud of small dots of my world of car repair. He was telling me something, if I had heard right, that made this little boy and myself a part of the huge, awe-inspiring human condition. I froze, and said. "Wait, wait. Say that again."

The little boy said, "Yes, and after she stabbed her little boy, she put him in the closet right over there."

Now that I was really listening with my heart, I heard something else in his voice; a strain I didn't think belonged in the voice of a four-year-old. It was there so intensely, that it became all too clear why he had to speak to a stranger wrestling with a muffler.

I lay there peering out at the boy, who was down on his knees looking at me. "Now, tell me again what happened to the little boy and his mommy?"

This time I realized that the ordinary tone I had mistaken for childish prattling, was the sound of fear and confusion. "The little boy's mommy was so sad and sick that she got a knife out of the kitchen. She was so sick she stabbed the little boy and put him in the closet and his blood came out," he answered.

I slid out from under the car and asked the boy to show me what he was talking about. He took my hand, led me around the car. There was no hesitation about which storage closet door he was talking about. He pointed directly to the one that had a sizeable streak of dried blood running out from the crack at the bottom of the door.

I ran to find the manager, and discovered that while I had been gone, a tenant had lost her senses, badly wounded her small son with a knife, and placed him in the closet in the garage. Fortunately, a rescue team found him and was able to save his life before he bled to death.

I went back to the little boy and let him tell me the story once again. When I really listened to him, it was clear he wanted assurance that this was an anomaly among the adult people in his life, and that other adults would protect him and guard him. The way to bring this assurance was to listen to him.

I remember this event every time I tell the story of Jesus passing people in the crowd and one woman reaching out to grab his garment, if even to just get the power she thought resided in the clothing he was wearing. That day a little boy reached out to grab my clothing, hoping for a healing of his fear. He needed someone who would be the bearer of the kind of assurance of loving care that Jesus gave to the world.

I could so easily have missed the feel of his little fingers tugging at my heart. It was a great lesson in my Christian life; one I never forgot. I remember it because it was the first time I sat down to honestly assess my need to listen more patiently, and to take the time to listen, so that I was able to see people in the bigger picture, and not get so hung up on the little dots of life.

In John 1:12, the Gospel writer says, "But to all who believed in Him, to them he gave the power to become the children of God." Simply stated, Jesus intended that we should do as he did. We should pass among each other knowing that we are given the power of love, compassion, attention, knowledge and support to help each other and become whole, and healed of the terrors that beset our lives. We have the perception to see people in the bigger picture of life. We need not be so fixated on the little dots of our important agendas, that we lose the ability to hear a little boy needing reassurance that all adults aren't monsters.

There is a great story told in *Stories and Parables for Preachers and Teachers* about an elementary school teacher who responded to her principal's invitation for all of the staff to write New Year's resolutions about how all of them could be better teachers and administrators in the year to come. He said that he would then post all of their work on the staff bulletin board. All of the teachers agreed to write resolutions, and when the resolutions were posted everyone gathered to see what kind of work had been produced.

But the teacher of our story discovered that her resolution was not posted. She went into a fit of anger. "He didn't put up my resolution. It was one of the first ones in. He doesn't care about me. That just shows what it's like around here." On and on she ranted.

The principal, who overheard this from his office, was mortified. He hadn't meant to exclude her resolution. Quickly rummaging through the papers on his desk he found it and immediately went to the bulletin board to put it up. The resolution read, *I resolve not let little things upset me.*

In such a state of anger, this person was not going to pass through life and feel the tug on her sleeve of a little boy, needing the healing assurance of an adult who would listen to him. When anger, obsessive interest in a task, overblown ambition, blind pride, crippling disbelief in one self, cause us to look at the dots, then we ignore the great clean sheet of the bigger picture God gives us in the assurance of Divine love.

Listen to Jesus who taught us that God has made us, and God has confidence in our ability to offer to humankind the healing grace we experienced in Christ. We are God's Christ bearers, made to pass through crowds and respond to the desperate touch. Let us look past the dots to the bigger picture faith paints for us. And be aware of who or what tugs at your clothing.

The Seasons of Faith

June 9, 2002

Hebrews 11:29-12:2

F aith is a powerful shaper of our lives. Helen Keller was born deaf, unable to speak, and blind. As a young girl, she met a loving, patient Christian teacher, who painstakingly led her to a point where she could communicate with the world beyond her disability. More than that, the teacher left Helen with the inner vision of the power of faith. It was that faith in God which directed her as an adult to a rich life of writing and public service. She was able to rise above her physical limits and pen this description of the faith that gave her such courage.

She wrote,

> "I believe that we can live on earth according to the teachings of Jesus, and that the greatest happiness will come to the world when man obeys His commandment 'Love one another.'
>
> I believe that we can live on earth according to the fulfillment of God's will, and that when the will of God is done on earth as it is done in heaven, every man will love his fellow man, and act toward them as he desires they should act toward him. I believe

that the welfare of each is bound up in the welfare of all.

I believe that life is given us so we may grow in love, and 1 believe that God is in me as the sun is in the color and fragrance of a flower, the Light in my darkness, the Voice in my silence.

I believe that only in broken gleams has the Sun of Truth yet shone upon men. I believe that love will finally establish the kingdom of God on earth, and that the cornerstones of that kingdom will be liberty, truth, brotherhood, and service."

Near the end of World War II, when the Allied forces swept across Germany, an army unit went searching for snipers in farm buildings and houses. At one abandoned house, almost a heap of rubble, searchers with flashlights found their way to the basement.

There, on a crumbling wall, a victim of the Holocaust had scratched a Star of David. And beneath it, in rough lettering, the message:

I believe in the sun-even when it does not shine.
I believe in love-even when it is not shown.
I believe in God-even when he does not speak.

The eleventh chapter of the book of Hebrews is a primer on the power of faith for the early Christian community. It begins with a definition of faith.

"Now faith is the assurance of things hoped for, the conviction of things not seen. Indeed, by faith our ancestors received approval. By faith we understand that the worlds were prepared by the word of God, so that what is seen was made from the things that are not visible."

In another part of the 11th chapter of Hebrews, the writer tells of the seasons of faith by reminding us of the great stories which helped create their faith tradition. These are the aspects or seasons of faith we should likewise expect in our lives.

The writer of Hebrews tells of the seasons of victory brought about by living out faith in God. He reminds his readers of the great story of Moses and the downtrodden band of ex-slaves who were on the run from their master in Egypt. When they were caught between the advancing power of war chariots and the sea of Reeds, they had faith in God to cross the marsh instead of surrendering. They were miraculously allowed to pass through the sea and its waters drowned the men and horses of the Pharaoh. This is the quintessential story of deliverance that gave the people of the Exodus the will to press on through the wilderness and into the land of promise.

Helen Keller's words are the words of one who experienced the victory of faith and a triumph of spirit over adversity. Faith gives its practitioners this ability. It gave Jesus the ability to see his fate ahead and the will to meet it without wavering.

During World War II an allied troop ship was struck by a torpedo. Life preservers were in short supply as the ship listed and started down to the bottom. Three sailors despaired because they knew that without life preservers they would surely die. Three chaplains were clinging to the listing wreck and they noticed the frightened seamen. So handing their preservers to the three sailors, the three chaplains gathered together for prayer near the highest point of the ship that was still visible. The chaplains were still there when the boat slipped beneath the waves. The three sailors they saved and the rest of the ship's survivors watched as the three chaplains went to their deaths in prayer. They had enough faith in the power of the resurrection to die for it and in their dying, they left behind a powerful, victorious legacy of faith in what it means to do as Jesus said, "Love your neighbor as though he were yourself."

God's Border Collies

April 21, 2002

Because I am a pliable father, I own a sheepdog named Montague. I have had him less than a year and despite my plans prior to his arrival, he has become a large part of my life. When he entered my life and home, I did not know much about sheep dogs, or border collies as they are also known, save for the fact that they were very human oriented. This means they care very much about what their human owner commands them to do and in an effort to please their human owners, they will work to do so. This is why we respectfully call them working dogs.

What I didn't realize was the herding instinct that is bred into them and the desire to keep little copies of their human master safe and sound, as they would any group of sheep.

One day, during my late wife's illness, we were very delighted to have close friends come to visit us and bring with them their twin children who were probably about three years old at the time. After playing and visiting with the children for a while I decided it was time for the kids to meet the dog. I assured them that Monty would like to meet them and they were filled with glee at the prospect of meeting a fun, playful doggie. They ran ahead of me through the house, and out of our French doors and onto the back deck.

Monty was sitting on the grass watching the house when the children emerged, laughing, onto the deck. As soon as he saw the children his head and ears came up. I could tell that these fast moving little children had his undivided attention. Before I could call out to him, Monty put his head down, crouched and charged. He was silent, but his eyes and face were so intensely focused on the two children that there was no doubt in the children's mind that this dog wanted them to move. In a flash they turned, streaked past me into the house with my sheep dog in hot pursuit. I followed behind horrified. The kids ran into the living room and leaped onto the couch, as Monty screeched to a halt in front of the couch. He sat on his haunches staring at them intently. Each time they moved, he moved, letting them know that they should stay put. It was clear that they were just where he thought they should be and that he thought that I would think the same.

Our friend who watched the dog herd her twins onto the couch and then keep them there, said laughingly, "Hey, do you want to rent him out for babysitting?"

What I have come to understand about my dog is that his nature is to do the bidding of his master. He is most intent when that bidding has to do with the care of living things his master wants to protect, guide, and nurture. Monty is happiest when he is living energetically in a way that fulfills his master's wishes. And I'm told that if I act as a loving master to this dog, he will have the confidence to herd animals much, much bigger than he.

To have faith in Christ, to live the Christian life is to understand that we are designed to be God's border collies in all of our endeavors. If we are in business it is we who should be cognizant of when a business deal needs to have someone speak out and look at it under the spotlight of moral scrutiny. You may not win the boardroom vote, nor win the approbation of those who worship only success, but you will know the victory of acting according to the nature God has imparted to your soul and placed in your heart. The wisdom of our Border collie nature is noted in the words of Confucius, the eastern sage, who said, "The superior person understands what is right; the inferior person understands what will sell."

It's time to be done with the passive metaphor of being the dim-witted flock of God. We are the Christian pack of God's border collies. We are by nature wired to do best when we are pleasing our master and seeking to do his will. We are happiest when we are herding life toward the kingdom instead of passively waiting for someone else to make use of what we have to offer. God gives us real work to do because God entrusts us with being the co-workers of Christ. Just like the master's love for her border collie, God's love even makes us able to herd things bigger than we are. You are created to be God's Border Collies. So do not huddle with the flock. Run with the Pack.

Heaven in Your Ears

November 9, 1997

1 Samuel 16:14-23 Acts 16;19-26

The restorative power of music has been long known by human beings. The story of Saul's mental affliction is a perfect example of this realization. When the great leader of the fledgling state of Israel fell into what we now know is clinical depression, he felt utterly cut off from God and human kind. Yet, somehow the melody from a harp would become the sound of the Spirit he had thought had abandoned him, and would help see him through another night.

When Paul and Silas healed a young girl of her mental delusions, which exploitative men were selling as predictions of the future, they found themselves in real trouble. The exploiters charged them with disturbing the peace and defying local customs. The magistrates had the two men beaten, their clothing savagely torn off of them and sent to prison. In the dark, bleeding, almost naked, the two men sought courage and comfort in their faith and they accessed that courage and comfort in song. Acts 16 says, "But about midnight Paul and Silas were praying and singing hymns to God, and the prisoners were listening to them."

Many years ago, a young man was caring for his sick mother at her house when he answered a phone call from a distant relative who had called unexpectedly, surprising him by breaking a silence his mother had imposed on all such family relationships years before. He instinctively knew that it couldn't be good news. It wasn't. He was told his father had died.

His father, the shadowy figure who had been divorced by his mother so many years ago, was the strange figure whom his mother seemed to hate and somehow love at the same time. To the boy, he was an elusive, far-off personage who would promise so much and deliver so little. His father's words haunted him: "We'll get together soon." "I'll be there for Christmas." "I'll be a little late." "Sorry, I'm tied up and won't see you this birthday." He wanted to call his father a failure and forget him, but he couldn't. He wanted to love him and forgive him, but he couldn't.

Now, caught in the half-light between these ultimate conclusions, his father had died. The boy went to school the next day and couldn't bring himself to tell anyone what had happened. To do so he would have had to say something about his dad and he didn't really know him. He would have had to say something about his mom, how she felt, why she was sick, or why he felt the way he did.

He was allowed to attend his father's Rosary, and for years afterwards could plainly recall the sounds of his father's casket being wheeled into the church. It had a squeaking wheel, which mournfully sang from one end of the mission Basilica to the other as it bore his dead father first into the Mass, and then out again. There were people there he had never seen and he knew he would never see them again. He wondered why they mourned and really wondered whether he was mourning.

After the service he was alone at home and buried himself in homework until he was too distracted to do any more. He went into his room, sat in the dark and turned on the radio.

Out of its buzzing speakers, straining to bring in a distant, lonely classic station came the words of Isaiah so wonderfully crafted into musical phrases by George Frederick Handel before the American Revolution. The boy's room was filled with the most powerful, mystical, redeeming, and hopeful sounds he had ever heard:

"Surely, He has born our grief, and carried our sorrow... He was wounded for our iniquities ... and the chastisement of our peace was upon Him." He had heard the words before, but somehow, framed by Handel 200 years before him, the words and soaring music cut through the fog in his soul like the piercing sound of a channel marker. He knew then that his grief and sorrow was being carried for him, and God would give him peace.

It was the height of the baroque in the ear of the music critic but it was heaven in the boy's ears. From that moment on, he was never again afraid to view the reality of his father's mortal shortcomings and, more importantly, his strengths.

Music inspires and redeems. Music reminds us that there are parts of our faith that cannot be put into words. Somehow this juxtaposition of sounds and words can do something for us that basic scholarship cannot.

Our worship of God can be joyfully and solemnly expressed in the artistic medium of music. The sacred music played on the harpsichord, organ, bells, drums and human voices span the periods from the Dark Ages to the modern age. It tells us that God is transmitted to us from sounds as stately as the hymns of Isaac Watts to the rhythms of Calypso. They are all valid expressions of God.

In 1746 John Fawcett was ordained as a Baptist Minister in

England and accepted a call to pastor a small and impoverished congregation in Wainsgate, located in Northern England. After spending several years at Wainsgate, where his salary was meager and his family growing, he received a call to the large and influential Carter's Lane Baptist Church in London to succeed the well-known pastor.

As the day for the scheduled departure from Wainsgate arrived, with the distraught parishioners gathered around the wagons, Mrs. Fawcett finally broke down and said, "John, I cannot bear to leave, I know not how to go!" "Nor can I either," said the saddened pastor. The order was soon given to unpack the wagons.

During one of his ensuing sermons Fawcett shared this hymn text with his congregation. It was one of a number of poems Fawcett had written and was printed under the title of Brotherly Love in 1782. It was the text to the familiar hymn. "Blessed be the tie that binds our hearts in Christian Love. The fellowship of kindred hearts is like to that above."

Though Fawcett became a sought-after preacher, scholar, and writer, and was again offered lucrative positions of great prestige elsewhere, he never left that small parish, dying there on July 25, 1817. It is interesting that though many of us have not known the content of Fawcett's life, his spirit has been conveyed to countless Christian souls through the music to which his poem was set, *Blessed be the Tie that Binds*.

When Fanny Cosby wrote the text of *All the Way My Savior Leads Me*, it came from the circumstances in her life. She was desperately in need of money, $5 to be exact, and she sat down and prayed earnestly over this matter, as was her custom. Within a few minutes a stranger appeared at her door with just the amount she needed. She wrote "I have no way of accounting for this, except to believe that God, in answer to my prayer, put it into the heart of this good man to bring the money. My first thought was, it is so wonderful the way the Lord leads me. I immediately wrote the poem and Dr. Lowry set it to music."

When Fanny Cosby speaks of God leading her, it is important to know that Fanny Cosby was blinded at the age of six weeks by improper medical treatment and was never able to see again. She married a blind musician, Alexander Van Alsyne, and became one of the gifted gospel hymn writers of her time, something she didn't even begin to do until her early forties.

Fanny Cosby, blind yet sighted by the light of Christ, somehow packs the joy, the hope, and the inspiration into more than words when her poem is set to music. It has inspired thousands of souls since that time, souls afflicted by inner blindness, seeking hope that says, "For I know whate'er befall me, Jesus doeth all things well."

Music is God's gift. Use it, study it, take it in, and enjoy it. It can heal you like the sounds of Handel healed the young high school student of the pain of his father's absence. I know it is true. I was that boy.

Seventy Times Seven

May 28, 2006

In the short time that I have left to preach in this pulpit as your pastor I want to deal with some of the things I hold to be essentially necessary for a spiritual life in general and a Christian life in particular.

The text from the sixth chapter of Luke sets the stage for the rule of the loving heart in Christian faith. From the teachings in these lessons comes the parable of the Good Samaritan, the Good Shepherd and the commandments about forgiving one another. These are the hardest disciplines of our faith; yet they yield the most fruit.

If one searches the Old Testament for examples of people asking forgiveness of each other for wrongful acts, one discovers that it was not a part of the religious tradition. They believed that God would forgive their sins without making them suffer as they might deserve, but there is nothing of any note in the writings about one person going to any great effort to forgive another. Indeed, in Jesus' day, the Jewish tradition taught that one should forgive another three times. After that, it was felt the forgiving would only become a source of unwitting support of wrongdoing.

It is clear that Jesus felt that if this rule were to be invoked against the authorities who treated his disciples so badly, they would never have hope of forgiveness before God. Yet from the cross he pled for forgiveness for all of those who sought his death.

So it is no wonder that Peter came to Jesus, Matthew tells us, asking how many times he was to forgive one who had wronged him. Should he increase the traditional number to twice as many and add one? Would seven be enough? The answer was no, it wasn't enough. Forgiveness was not a formula. It was connected to an entire way of life; a way of viewing human endeavor and human nature. Jesus pointed out that to really grow in the love of God one had to prepare himself to forgive endlessly. This is the meaning of Jesus telling Peter that one is to forgive 70 times 7 times.

Then he told Peter a parable. A servant owed his master 10,000 talents. This was a staggering amount of money. A laborer made about a denarii a day and it took 6,000 denarii to add up to a talent. The servant owed his king 60 million denarii or the wages from 60 million days of a laborers work.

Clearly the servant owed a debt he could never possibly pay in all of his lifetime or in several lifetimes to come. When his master sought to sell him and his possessions in order to recoup at least a miniscule fraction of the debt, the servant pled for mercy and time to pay off the loan. It was empty pleading, since it was a hopeless undertaking. Yet, somehow his pleading affected the master and touched his heart. Instead of taking any of the servant's property or selling him off, the master simply forgave the entire debt and wiped the slate clean. He told the servant that he was free to start over.

After rejoicing mightily at this great gift of forgiveness, the servant ran into a fellow servant who owed him 100 denarii, a 100 days of labor. It was no small debt given the servant's meager wages, but after what had been done for him, it was truly insignificant. Instead of passing along the spirit of forgiveness, the servant demanded the payment on the spot. When it was not forthcoming, he signed a warrant for the man's arrest so that the poor man could work off the debt in debtor's prison. It is no wonder that the master was incensed when he heard what the servant had done. He retracted his act of forgiveness and asked for the debt to be paid in full.

This is a serious matter Jesus brings before us, telling us that the nature of God is so filled with grace, mercy and forgiveness that God's will intends that we act toward one another as God acts toward us. This matter is so important that it is included in the Lord's Prayer, which clearly tells us that we will be forgiven in the same measure that we forgive others.

It is one thing to forgive small things, like a little lie someone tells about us, or a small amount of money someone wrongfully takes from us. But it is quite another matter to forgive the more heinous acts even when the perpetrator honestly pleads for forgiveness and means to amend his/her actions in the future.

Simon Wiesenthal once related that as a young Jew he was taken from a death camp to a makeshift army hospital. He was led to the bedside of a Nazi soldier whose head was completely swathed in bandages. The dying Nazi blindly extended his hand toward Simon, who had been identified to him as a Jew. In a cracked whisper the dying soldier began to speak, confessing having participated in the burning alive of an entire village of

Jews. The soldier was terrified of dying with this burden of guilt, and begged absolution from a Jew who might represent those he slaughtered. Having listened to the Nazi's story for several hours -- torn between compassion and horror -- Simon finally walked out of the room without speaking and without forgiving. For the rest of his life that moment haunted Simon Wiesenthal. Should he have forgiven?

When Jesus was being tortured on a cross while his false accusers hurled invectives and mockery at him, he turned his eyes to heaven and begged the God forgive them for their sin and ignorance.

When Corrie Ten Boom, a devout Christian encountered this same kind of difficulty after the war, the story of Jesus on the cross weighed heavily upon her. Corrie had suffered through the death and humiliation and total cruelty of the German Concentration Camp at Ravensbruck. Her sister had died from the planned deprivation of the camp as had thousands of others. During a speech before a group of German Christians in Munich in 1947, Corrie had proclaimed that when Christians confess their sins God casts them into the deepest ocean forever and they are gone forever. After the speech, a balding man in a gray overcoat and a brown felt hat clutched between his hands approached her. There was something familiar about him. Suddenly she remembered who he was: He had been one of the crueler of the guards at Ravensbruck. The man stood before her his hand thrust out. He said,

> "A fine message, Fraulein. How good it is to know that, as you say, our sins are at the bottom of the sea. You mentioned Ravensbruck in your talk; I was a guard there. But since that time, I have become a Christian. I know

that God has forgiven me for the cruel things that I did there, but I would like to hear it from your lips as well, Fraulein," again the hand came out, "will you forgive me?"

It took every ounce of her experience and belief in just what God is and what forgiveness is truly all about to extend her hand. She gazed at the man who had so loyally worked for the Nazis who had murdered her sister and thousands like her and savaged her life for years and said, "With all my heart, brother, you are forgiven."

I have a very close friend who once met Corrie after that fateful day. It was in the late 1950s and he was a young boy suffering from a malady in his eye that was threatening him with blindness. There was great concern about the nature of his recovery from the medical procedures that were trying to correct his problem. Corrie Ten Boom was visiting families connected to his church and well meaning parishioners had asked her to call on my friend in the hospital.

My friend remembers her warmth and sincerity. She laid her hand on his eyes ever so gently, as she spoke and prayed a very simple prayer. He remembered comforting warmth radiating from her hand into his face, something he couldn't really describe fully, even as an adult. The next day all of the people attending him were astounded at the healing that had happened overnight. They couldn't explain it but were all too glad to simply accept it and move on.

People who have the capacity to forgive like that, who have truly learned what to bind onto a human conscience and what to let go of, have spirits that heal. Corrie Ten Boom didn't present herself as a healer before or after this experience. She was just a vessel of God's forgiving grace, a human testament to what grace can and does do in a life that touches other lives. My friend remembered as much about the calming nature of her presence as he did that mysterious physical warmth that apparently healed his eye.

A minister wrote in a forum on forgiving:

> "For twenty-one years I had been harboring intense anger against my father. Like a fiery bed of simmering coals, my anger burned deep within me, where only those closest to me could see it. But now, I suddenly knew that I needed to forgive my father, at least for my own well being.
>
> I was having a phone conversation with a close ministerial friend. We were developing a talk for clergy and laity on the subject of Christian forgiveness. The more we talked, the more we realized that our topic was complex and often misunderstood, even by clergy.
>
> As usual, our conversation turned personal. I had confided the painful story of my father to my friend. My parents separated bitterly when I was in high school. My father turned against his three sons. He circulated a letter of vicious lies in town to destroy our reputations and moved to Canada to avoid paying child support.
>
> I last saw my father in 1964, when I was sixteen. After that, I spoke with him only twice. The last time, he claimed he was not my father and threatened to harm me if I ever contacted him again. Years later, in 1990, I

learned that my father had died--and changed his last name!

It was now 1993. My friend knew my pain. In a gentle way we debated our subject over the phone. Citing Jesus' words, "If there is repentance, you must forgive," I clung to my anger and the reverse idea that Christians need not forgive, when there is no repentance.

Finally, in this conversation he said, "Here's what I'm concerned about. What happens to me when I don't forgive?" This time his words struck me. Beyond my clinging to any proof text, his words spoke to my soul.

It was difficult at first, but that afternoon in my study, I decided to set out on a journey of forgiveness. For me, this became a daily journey of the heart. It was a journey of trying, with God's help, to let go of all those fiery coals I had been holding against my father. As I now realized, those coals were burning me!

My journey included prayer, self-reflection, sharing my journey with others, and my desire to be freed from re-living these nightmares of my past. Above all, I trusted our God of love and forgiveness to go with me, no matter how arduous my journey. Weeks passed into months. Slowly my intense anger began to cool. Finally, after more than two years, a day came when I realized I no longer bore ill will toward my father. With God's help, I had forgiven him!

I still considered his actions to be wrong. But even so, what a difference! After all those years of simmering anger, I had come to a place where I felt a real sense of peace with my father's memory--and myself. This experience touched my life and faith deeply."

Jesus once told a story about a young man who came in from the fields sweaty, tired, and hungry after a day's hard labor. He was chagrined to hear that his brother, who had run off with a third of his father's money, had returned home despicably poor, having squandered all he had in loose, and irresponsible living. Now he was home, begging for his father to just let him work in the stables as a hired hand. Instead his father had thrown his arms around him and welcomed him home with great joy.

His older brother declined to join the party his father was throwing for his errant sibling. When his father begged him to join in he replied bitterly.

"I remember how he treated you and me. I remember how he abandoned us and took his inheritance with him. Well, I'm still here working. I don't ask for special favors or to withdraw my support from the farm for my own selfish desires. And what do I get for my loyalty and hard work-- An invitation to a welcome home party for my flaky brother."

Yes, that is what the father wanted. He wanted this brother to let go of the past and start over. The contrition of his younger brother meant something. It deserved the act of forgiveness and he wanted his elder son to understand that the blessing was in the son's return, whatever his circumstances. It removed all doubt that the forgiveness he had already granted would ever be asked for or accepted.

Peace and life affecting wisdom are not forged from acts of the mind alone. They are begun in the mind, heart and soul then forged in actions that pay great prices to obtain huge gains of grace, loving kindness, wisdom, and spiritual peace. I believe that in the end only these acts can release us from the prisons of both righteous and unrighteous anger. Though we wish revenge to be sweet, in the end it is only confining and damaging to our souls and the purposes of God's peace that passes understanding.

Yes, Peter, we are to forgive 70 times 7 times, endlessly, relentlessly. We are the servants owing our master untold years of hard labor and been forgiven our debt. Is it no wonder that we pray as we do:

Father, forgive us our debts as we forgive our debtors
Amen.

The Compassionate Life

June 4, 2006

The day of Pentecost is the birthday of the church. We traditionally celebrate it with communion, and a reading of the Pentecost story. To acknowledge the outpouring of the Holy Spirit on that day, let us explore together what I think is essential to a full spiritual life in Christ; that is to commit oneself to compassion by consistently and constantly involving oneself in the discipline of being compassionate. I believe that without this - this immersing ourselves in the endeavor to be compassionate - there is no spiritual life. You have to perform it, if you want the life.

In the eighth chapter of John we read where the authorities confronted Jesus on the matter of adultery. They wanted to make him struggle with this because they wanted him to refute the law. They said to him, "Well, here's a woman caught in adultery. You know what the law of Leviticus says-- she is to be executed." But Jesus had taught, "I say to anyone who looks upon the spouse of another lustfully, has already committed adultery in his or her heart." That's what Jesus taught. So how would he balance his teaching with the desires of the authorities? Pick up the stone and let the stoning begin?

I observed a similar conflict when I was nineteen years old and a college student in Los Angeles. It was there I experienced my first whiplash. Although it was extremely mild and involved only the slightest little twinges of pain that passed quickly, it was caused by something far less serious than a little fender-bender from the rear end in an automobile accident.

It was a warm spring day and I decided I needed a haircut, so I left the college campus where I was living and ventured down into the town of Westwood, a community on the edge of the campus in Los Angeles. I found a barbershop and I was ushered into an empty chair. I could see people dressed in all sorts of summery garb through the big plate glass window. The girls from my college were dressed in shorts and halters - some a little more revealing than others. The intent was to be cool and, for some, stylish.

The barber seemed to be inordinately tense. Halfway through the hair cut, he began to mumble under his breath, saying things like: "I don't believe it. Get a load of that. I wonder if she would dress like that if her Mom were here." Clearly the man was getting progressively steamed up over the scanty dress that the co-eds were wearing as they passed the Barber Shop. The more he muttered, the louder he became. I began to feel that the impropriety of the young women's apparel wasn't what was really driving all of his excitement. He was getting himself all steamed up by something darker in his head - something about what he himself desired. His almost violent talk was an expression of his desire, not of his judgment, and it was making me pretty nervous.

It wasn't long before the guy started to let his tension and excitement travel from his mind into his hands and into the clippers he was using on my head. I could hear the click, click, click of the scissors accelerating as he talked about women and their improper and suggestive attire. His face was flushed, and as he glanced out the window with all those jerky movements, I feared he was concentrating a little more on what was going on outside on the sidewalk instead of on my head. Suddenly the scissors stopped dead and he cried out right in my ear: "Look at that!" Before I knew what was happening, the chair was swiveled to the right at warp speed and it stopped just as suddenly as if a rocking chair had been struck by an asteroid. My face was facing out the window but my eyeballs were still pointing toward the mirror. It took a millisecond for them to catch up with my eye sockets, swing past them to the other side and finally bounce back. During all that action, my neck sustained its first experience with whiplash.

Obviously, the barber wanted me to see some terrible indiscretion of dress, but all I could see were my classmates. Yet, I saw in my mind's eye more clearly than I saw with my eyes, a person that would fit what Jesus was saying about committing adultery in his heart. His cloak of desire clashed with the message of his wedding ring. If Jesus had been there, and not been the bodily representation of the great compassion of God, he would have evoked the law of Leviticus and we all would have gotten up with the scissors and -- well, you know the rest.

The Pharisees in the passage from the book of John had it right according to the Leviticus code. The Law of Moses made it clear that adultery would be punishable by death in Jesus' time, and in the case of the woman who the authorities so self-righteously dragged before Jesus, it was clear that she and her consort had broken that law. It was also clear to Jesus that this frightened, guilt-ridden woman whom the authorities had brought before him (you wonder where the other half was) did NOT deserve death. Nor did the barber deserve death for harboring thoughts that were hidden, even from him, in all that anger.

We'll never know what Jesus was writing in the dirt while he was being harangued by the Pharisees to impose death on the adulteress. I have no doubt this woman could not believe it when Jesus said to the crowd, "Let he who is without sin, cast the first stone." It became very quiet when Jesus bent over and wrote in the dirt. One by one, the accusers began to slink away, probably asking "I wonder what he knows? Does he know something about me? Maybe the first stone would be cast at me". When they had all gone, Jesus stood up and looked at the woman. "Has no one condemned you?" he asked. She answered, ""No." Jesus looked at her with compassion and said, "Nor do I. Go and sin no more."

Considering this level of compassion some will complain and say, "But, that seems like permission to sin and we can't be permissive." Yes, you can be. And sometimes you cannot. There are no compassion formulas in human life. We have all said, "I will never give this or that to my children when they get older!" And then, of course we do. "I will never in my life say ___ " and then we do. No, the formulas don't work. Wisdom does. And that comes from walking in the shoes of Christ, of having the spirit of God alive within you. Having compassion is the willingness to see the world as God sees it. To see what is wrong and yet also see into the complex web of human need, pain, confusion, pride, arrogance, diminishment, and self-hatred. If we take the time, have the grace and pay the price to look deeply enough, it's there.

Jesus told people the laws of the prophets were summed up in the rule that we should love God and our neighbors as ourselves.

The faultfinders, the hair-splitters said, "Now, define neighbor." Jesus answered with a story the story of the Good Samaritan. He explained that all the people who passed this poor, broken man who had been left on the side of the road by thieves to die had reasons for not showing compassion. It was the least likely person of all, the one who had the most reason not to care or have compassion, who arrived on the scene. He was a Samaritan held in contempt by Jews of the time, just as the Samaritans held the Jews in contempt. But when he saw the injured Jew he had total compassion. He not only dressed his wounds and saw to it that the man recovered, he paid the bill. He didn't leave a card behind saying, "Get a hold of me so you can say thank you later." He didn't leave anything behind except the sense that somewhere in all of life's confusion, hatred and despair there was hope!

Now, just as then, this world hungers for both righteousness and compassion and our neighbor is the world. This is a piece of wisdom spread throughout religious experiences all over the globe. It's been around for at least six thousand years; and not just among Christians but among other faiths as well.

Something sacred blows into our souls; we put our egos behind us and say, "What is the harmony of the divine?" And this answer of compassion appears over and over in Christian teaching, as well as in the canons of the Hindu, Buddhist, and others. So it was that Jesus said, "Love your enemies. Pray for those who persecute you so that you may be the children of your father who is in heaven. Don't judge, lest you be judged."

You see that same compassionate spirit expressed in the **Garland Sutra** of Buddhism. It is written: "I should be like the sun shining universally on all without seeking thanks or rewards, able to take care of all sentient beings even if they are bad. Never giving up on my vows on this account. Not abandoning all sentient beings just because one sentient being is evil."

In the Ramayana, a part of the Hindu Canon, there is this statement: "A superior being does not render evil for evil. This is a maxim one should observe: The ornament of virtuous persons is their conduct. One should never harm the wicked or the good or even criminals. For who is without fault?"

Compassion is illustrated in the Islamic Hadith of Bukhari with these words according to Anas: After the messenger of God said, "Help your brother whether he is an oppressor or oppressed." Anas replied to him, "O Messenger of God, a man who is oppressed, I am ready to help. But how does one help an oppressor?" He answered, "By hindering him in doing wrong."

Similarly, Jesus, out of compassion for the poor who were being cheated out of their money by the currency changers in the temple, knotted a rope and turned it into a whip and drove the exchange agents out of the temple. In that act, he showed compassion for both the oppressor and the oppressed.

Compassion is a discipline. It is born of daily meditation upon how the image of Christ lives in every person, despite all the willful and imposed layers of human thought and emotion that try to suppress it. Compassion is the discipline of controlling the ego so the eye of perceptive divinity can see clearly. Compassion is the companion of redemption for it sees all beings as redeemable. We can gain a trace of this compassion by being empathetic, kind-hearted, forgiving and full of grace for those that we know and like. But we will never find it developing robustly until we practice it in acts of merciful understanding of those we don't exactly love. Practice compassion on those who really annoy us or do things quite differently than we do - those who seek a different path than ours – who have a different dogma or none at all.

Compassion directs that I understand that there was something burrowing into the soul of that barber who gave me my first case of whiplash. Somewhere in his frustrated, self-righteous anger, there was something Jesus would have found redeemable. Jesus made it clear that unless we seek a discipline that can love the folk who are repulsive in our lives we will have unfulfilled compassion. Where do you start? Well, maybe you start by not judging anyone.

I found great compassion displayed in the movie, "Bang the Drums Slowly". It's about a baseball team that was on a long losing streak, and as is the case with so many of us guys, when things start going bad, we start criticizing each other. The team was especially tormenting the young catcher. After a while it became known that this young catcher had caught something besides pitched balls. He had caught cancer. As time went on, it was obvious that he was not going to survive the illness. As he tried to finish out the year, a few of his teammates befriended him and tried to make him more comfortable by doing acts of compassion. Soon, the entire team began to do the same thing. As they stopped ridiculing the catcher, they began to leave off ragging on each other. Interestingly enough, they began to win ballgames because they started acting like a team. In fact, they rose from the cellar into the heights. What they really wanted to do was make life meaningful for that young catcher and they did. In turn they made it meaningful for themselves and they rose to the top.

The catcher died at the end of the movie. The narrating player of the story reflected on his friend and what had happened after the funeral. He ended by saying something like this. "I don't know why all of this had to happen. I don't know the meaning of a lot of things that go down in life, but as for me, I don't pick on anyone anymore."

Where does the discipline of the Christ's compassion start? It can start where the ball players started. It can start by not heaping scorn and ridicule on other people or yourself. It can start with prayer, reflection and forgiveness. As a result, I bet you will start winning ballgames.

Our Town

June 11, 2006
Last Sunday before Retirement

Before I begin talking about the scripture and really start the sermon, I want to remind you that for many, many years that I've been the pastor here, I have looked for illustrations out of my life to add a little bit more of the stories of scripture. I have mined many stories from my childhood and the experiences I shared with my older brother. I am reminded of a story of a foster sister I once had whom we called Big Shirley. At one time Big Shirley threatened to pound my brother and me into the ground and we were convinced that she could do it. She was not a happy child and she was older and taller than the rest of us.

One day there was an altercation out in the yard and I watched my brother being terrorized by Big Shirley and I could tell that he was *WINDING UP*. The next thing I knew he had decided to test the mettle of Big Shirley. He popped her one and she went down like a big tree. Crack! And that was the end of the legend of Big Shirley. I will never forget it.

Well, those stories were there probably because the companion of my childhood who believed in me so much and braved so many giants for me has been my brother, my biggest fan, who made me believe in myself when I was little and afraid. He's here today. I just want to say thank you, Jack.

When I was in high school I had a friend named Susan McIntyre. She was very bright, very shy and very intense. Her blond hair and fair skin was eye-catching and her shy intensity always made her seem as if there were a lot more going on in her head than came out her mouth. Her quiet intensity was an interesting mix with her gentleness that avoided outright conflict and social discomfort whenever possible. She was a bit of a loner and didn't have a great many friends. I knew her because we were both interested in writing and as well as having classes together, we both wrote for the school newspaper. We also belonged to the same church; she by family ties to Scotland through her father who no longer attended church with her.

One Sunday I was sitting in church watching Mr. Stewart's hand appear above the screen from where he directed the choir while he played the organ, when Susan McIntyre slid into the pew beside me. We greeted each other. No hugs. Egad! She was just my friend. In 1959 a hug would have been telegraphed everywhere in teenage land.

Ahead of us a woman had placed her coat over the back of the pew. Its collar was a sort of animal fur, a soft, longhaired reddish brown color. There was a vibrant, reflected fire in the color of the fur. It looked so soft, so alive and it caught Susan's attention.

Through the early part of the service I noticed Susan, looking at that collar. Her gaze seemed to massage the soft fur, follow its contour, and scrutinize its richness and beauty.

While the Rev. Russell Prentice called for prayer, Susan reached out and ever so gently touched the fur, pressing it softly, then withdrew her hand. Her cheeks were scarlet, as if she were embarrassed. I could see a string of thoughts, her eyes bright with glee as a great smile crept over her face. She withdrew her hand and held it momentarily in her other hand and I could almost feel her touch. She never knew I saw her. I watched the scarlet fade from her cheeks, while thinking, "Susan McIntyre .. Boy, is she out of her mind." What an unseeing idiot I was at 17 years of age.

When I was older I could look back on her action with more depth. I could appreciate that moment of tactile pleasure she had stolen for herself and the delight it must have given her.

A woman once touched Jesus the way Susan McIntyre touched that fur collar hanging over the back of the pew. It was the rule in Jewish society at that time that women didn't accost men in public that were not known to them. The woman was suffering from constant, energy draining, blood flows from serious menstrual issues. For twelve years she had fought it, using all her meager resources hoping to be cured, but every proposed remedy had failed. This was her chance to get near someone who seemed to be able to do what others had not been able to do.

In the pressing crowd of people, jostling each other trying to get close so they could hear and be heard, she was able to get just close enough. And just like Susan McIntyre, she secretly stretched out her hand toward Jesus' robe and though her soul was filled with an intense, desperate need to touch, like Susan, she touched the garment ever so gently, and then quickly withdrew her hand. I've no doubt that like Susan, one could see a flood of thoughts cross her face as the touch ran up her fingers, through her brain, into her body and ignited the cure.

It must have shocked her when Jesus turned about, sequentially looking into everyone's eyes asking, seeking, "Who touched me? Someone just touched me. Who was it?" How could he notice this touch? Even the disciples were perplexed that in a crowd of pushy men Jesus had recognized a particular touch of desperate need. Jesus was always aware, attentive to the moment. His soul was attuned to the sacred, while he set aside the non-sacred as an attentive second priority.

Jesus lets us know in this story and in his teaching that people who seek God need to pay attention to the sacred in the common matters of everyday living. One can indeed ascend to the heights, think and feel lofty thoughts. But from those heights one will never taste the water of the rivers that feed the mighty river below, nor see the ground as an owl risks its life to protect its young buried in a hole in the forest floor.

A spiritual life must learn attention to the moment. Without this attention, the moment blends into the patterns driven by desire, judgment, fear, and ambition. Faith is the conviction that the moment is filled with the holy and Christian faith affirms this over and over again.

Saints and sages of all of our faiths have learned this lesson. As they meditate, they drive from their consciousness all diversions from the present moment, giving them an ability to just be in the moment, letting its sacred content fill them with light. The results are stunning: patience, magnanimity, an ability to even overcome pain and hunger, and many other blessings.

In 1938, Thornton Wilder's play *Our Town* was performed for the first time. It was destined to be a classic play, hailed as a hallmark of American Literature. But it started out to mixed reviews. John Gassner in *One Act Play Magazine* dismissed the play as "devoid of developed situations". The critic in *Time Magazine* praised its use of what it called "Chinese methods in its use of scenery," then said, "but nevertheless the third act is full of disappointing mysticism and high flown speculation."

The point of the play was that the most holy of moments is the present moment with all of its commonness; that holy and beautiful sacredness is often lost to humans who are so busy trying to see beyond the horizon that they miss the here and now.

In the play, a narrator who acts something like a good angel calls forth scenes in the common life of people of Grover's Corners, New Hampshire at the beginning of the 20th century. We see the life of the Webb family and the Gibbs family. Dr. Gibbs' family lives directly across the path from the Webb family. They are close enough so that young George Gibbs can see young Emily Webb doing her homework through her bedroom window, and they can talk to each other easily when their windows are open. Their lives unfold in small town, rural America with all of the discussion of the weather and one another, and the humdrum of daily life.

George and Emily fall in love, marry, and build a life on a fine farm. Emily dies in childbirth and the last act of the play sees her as a ghost, among the ghosts sitting on the hill at the cemetery, patiently but expectantly looking for something in the future yet to happen. Wilder does not begin to tell us what that might be. Emily asks the stage manager to let her live again a day in her life and so she does. But instead of feeling wonderful, she finds herself amazed at the realization of how people are so unaware of how literally crammed with terrific beauty and meaning the most common moments are.

She says of all of the events of earth, so common in the moment, yet so filled with fire like the light glowing in the fur hanging in front of Susan McIntyre's gaze:

> "I didn't realize...
> So all that was going on and we never noticed.
> Take me back - up the hill- to my grave.
> But first: Wait!
> One more look.
> Good-bye, good-bye world.
> Good-bye Grover's Corners.
> Goodbye Mama, Papa.
> Good-by to clocks ticking and Mama's sunflowers
> and food and coffee and new-ironed dresses and hot
> baths. and sleeping and waking up.
> O, Earth, you're too wonderful to realize you."

Then looking toward the stage manager she asks abruptly through her tears: "Do any human beings ever realize life while they live it--every, every minute?"

Time Magazine's critic sniffed at the play's mysticism and high-flown speculation. Most likely it was referring to the congregation of spirits, waiting. It appears the highest-flying speculation at which the magazine turned up its cynical nose was the speech by the narrator or stage manager as he introduced the cemetery where the spirits sat waiting.

In this speech he says:

"Now there are some things we all know, but we don't take'm out and look at'm very often. We all know that something is eternal. And it ain't houses and it ain't names, and it ain't earth, and it ain't even the stars. Everybody knows in his or her bones that something is eternal, and that something has to do with human beings. All the greatest people ever lived have been telling us that for five thousand years and yet you'd be surprised how people are always losing hold of it. There's something way down deep that's eternal about every human being."

To store up for ourselves treasures in heaven isn't to look beyond what is here and now, crammed into the moment. It is rather an act of letting go of the judgments and ego that keep us from seeing the holy fires contained in the common moments of life.

If our eyes are spiritually trained they will be able to detect light, even in the darkest moments. Like night vision goggles they will turn sky glow into lamplight, and starlight into amazing incandescence. In failure, they will see promise that should be celebrated eagerly; in the moment of boredom they will discover interest, and in banality they will find mystery. Truly the eye is the lamp of the body, as Jesus said, "One must be attentive to its development and to its use. In this way we truly are awake and attentive to the moment."

Sometimes we blind our attention with ego and fear. The glowing fires of the holy in the moment are dimmed when we are too caught up in our judgments and our plans beyond the horizon. To strive first for the kingdom of God is to pay attention to the place of that eternal mystery the stage manager is talking about.

It takes work to get it out of our bones and into our vision of the moment. It takes meditation, contemplation, action and choices about the use of time and resource. But it can be done and it works.

When I was 17, I saw the moment through the foggy filters of my young man's chemistry, and ego, and self-interest. When I viewed Susan McIntyre's nervous fascination through all of that busyness of the moment, I didn't know what to make of her. I couldn't understand her solitariness, her hesitation in being a friend to many, and her fascination with beauty.

But after years of working to clean all of those filters, I see that moment so differently. I wish I had just said,

"Susan, what does the fur feel like?"

The Kingdom of God is now.

   Be Awake.
     Be Attentive.
       Be Still
         And know that God is Lord of the Moment
          And speaks in it.
                    Amen.

*I officiated at Jack's and Sheila's wedding. We continue to maintain a
very close relationship as adults.*

Rev. William (Bill) E. Nebo was born in Los Angeles County, California. Bill attended the University of California at Los Angeles and graduated with a Bachelors' Degree in philosophy in 1960. After studying at the San Francisco Theological Seminary where he earned his Master of Divinity degree, he was ordained in the Presbytery of Los Angeles in 1968. He served at the First United and Portalhurst Presbyterian Churches as an Assistant Pastor until 1972. After serving for four years as an Assistant and Associate Pastor at the Livermore Presbyterian Church in Livermore, California, he became its Senior Pastor and remained there until his retirement in 2006.

He was married for thirty years to his partner, Jean and they had two children, Valerie and Christopher. After Jean's death he married Jane Sheridan who brought her two sons, Kursten and Justen, into their life together. Currently he shares the care of his beloved Border collie, Monty with his daughter, Valerie, and granddaughter, Anna Jean.

Bill has and continues to have an abiding interest in bioethics and sits on the Institutional Review Board of Lawrence Livermore National Laboratory, the Bioethics Committee and Institutional Review Board of Valley Care Hospital, and the Human Subjects of Research Working Group of the Department of Energy.

Printed in the United States
200233BV00003B/1-177/A

9 780979 992902